VESTIGES

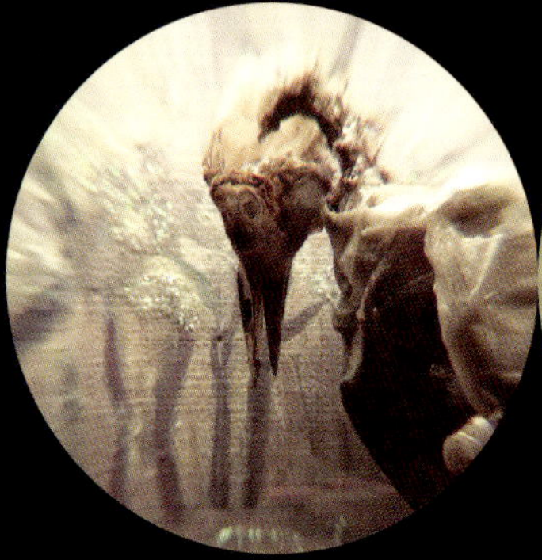
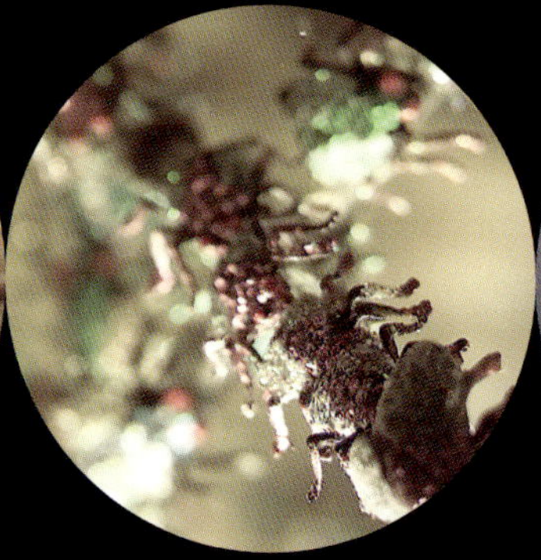
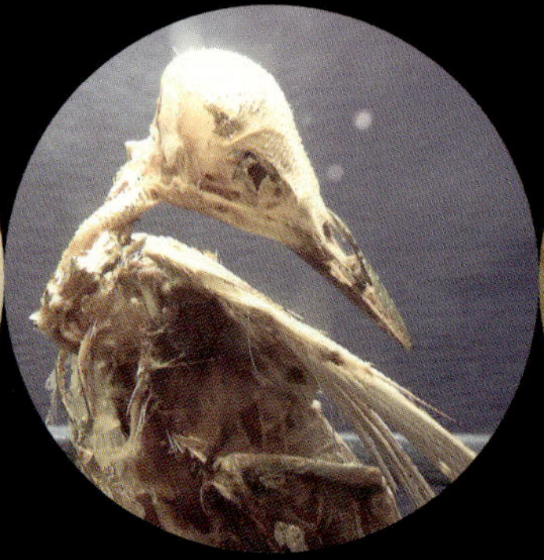
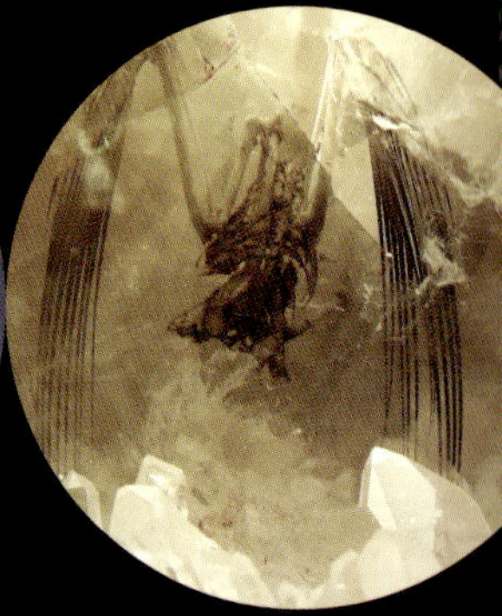

SHIRLEY BROWN

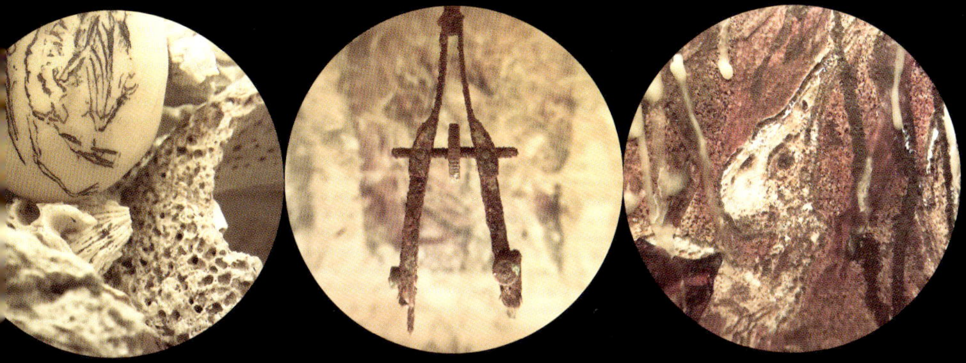

VESTIGES

Curated by Cathy Mattes

Essays by Cathy Mattes and Mary Reid

The Winnipeg Art Gallery

May 28 – July 31, 2005

Art Gallery of Southwestern Manitoba

August 25 – October 8, 2005

Library and Archives Canada Cataloguing in Publication

Brown, Shirley, 1943-
Shirley Brown : vestiges / curated by Cathy Mattes ; essays
by Cathy Mattes and Mary Reid.

Co-published by the Art Gallery of Southwestern Manitoba.

Catalogue of an exhibition held at the Winnipeg Art Gallery, May 28-Jul. 31, 2005,
and at the Art Gallery of Southwestern Manitoba, Aug. 25-Oct. 8, 2005.
Includes bibliographical references.

ISBN 0-88915-232-2

1. Brown, Shirley, 1943- —Exhibitions. 2. Civilization, Ancient, in art—
Exhibitions. I. Mattes, Cathy, 1974- II. Reid, Mary, 1972- III. Winnipeg Art Gallery
IV. Art Gallery of Southwestern Manitoba V. Title. VI. Title: Vestiges.

N6549.B765A4 2005 709'.2 C2005-902318-X

Curator: Cathy Mattes, Art Gallery of Southwestern Manitoba
Project Manager: Mary Reid, Curator of Contemporary Art and Photography, WAG
Editor: Jenny Gates
Proofreader: Heather Mousseau, WAG
Photographer: Ernest Mayer, WAG
Designer: Frank Reimer
Printer: Kromar Printing Ltd.

Printed in Canada

Financial assistance for this exhibition has been provided by the W.H. & S.E. Loewen Foundation.
Supported by the Canada Council for the Arts and the Manitoba Arts Council

THE WINNIPEG ART GALLERY
Involving People In The Visual Arts

ART GALLERY OF
SOUTHWESTERN MANITOBA

The Canada Council for the Arts since 1957 | Le Conseil des Arts du Canada depuis 1957

Manitoba Arts Council | Conseil des arts du Manitoba

FRONT COVER:
Cat. 1 *Untitled, Box #1* (detail) 2004

BACK COVER:
Cat. 22 *Untitled, Box #22* (detail) 2003

INSIDE COVERS:
Cat. 31 *Untitled, Box #31* (detail) 2003

OPPOSITE PAGE:
Cat. 15 *Untitled, Box #15* (detail) 2003

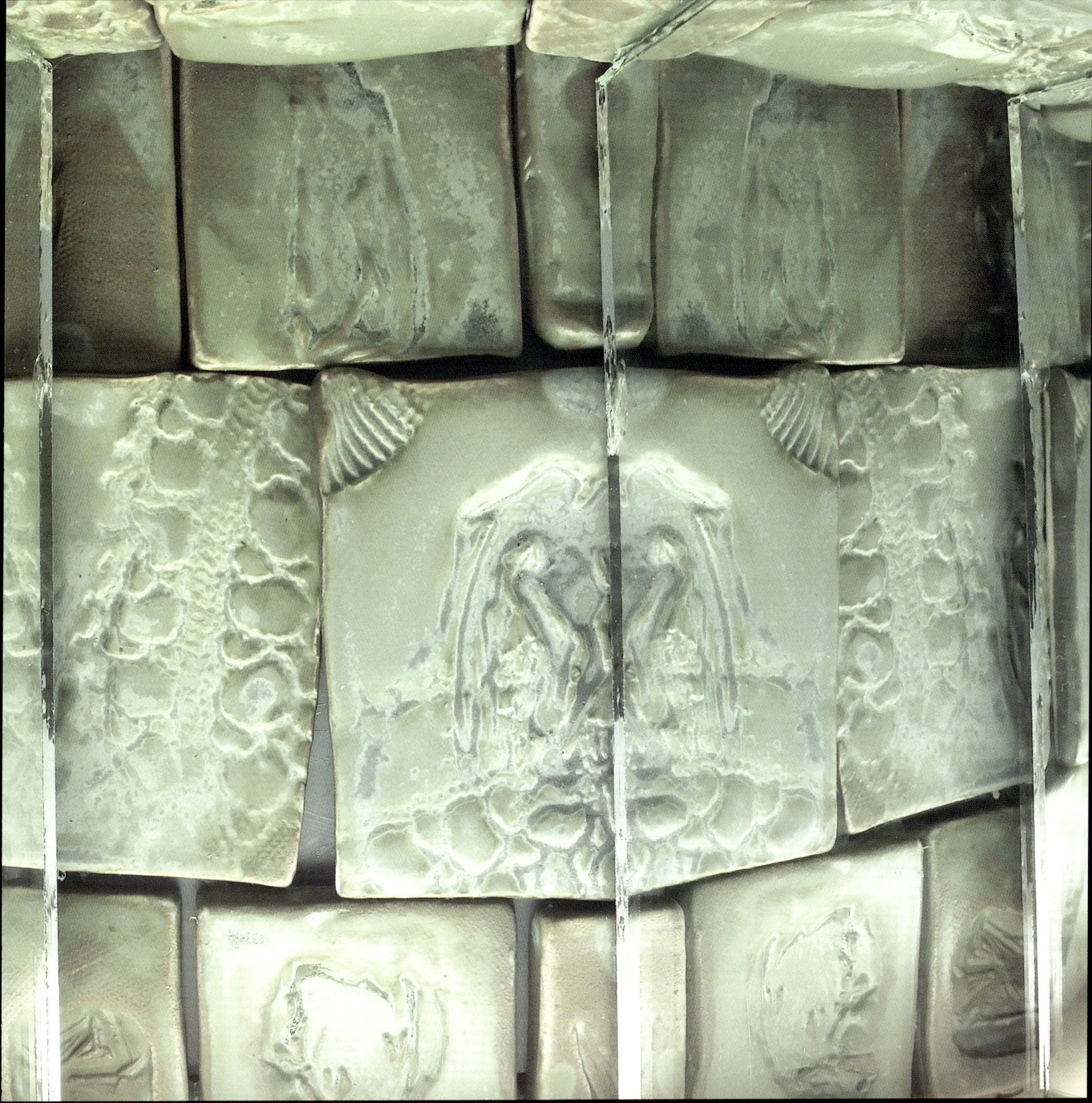

CONTENTS

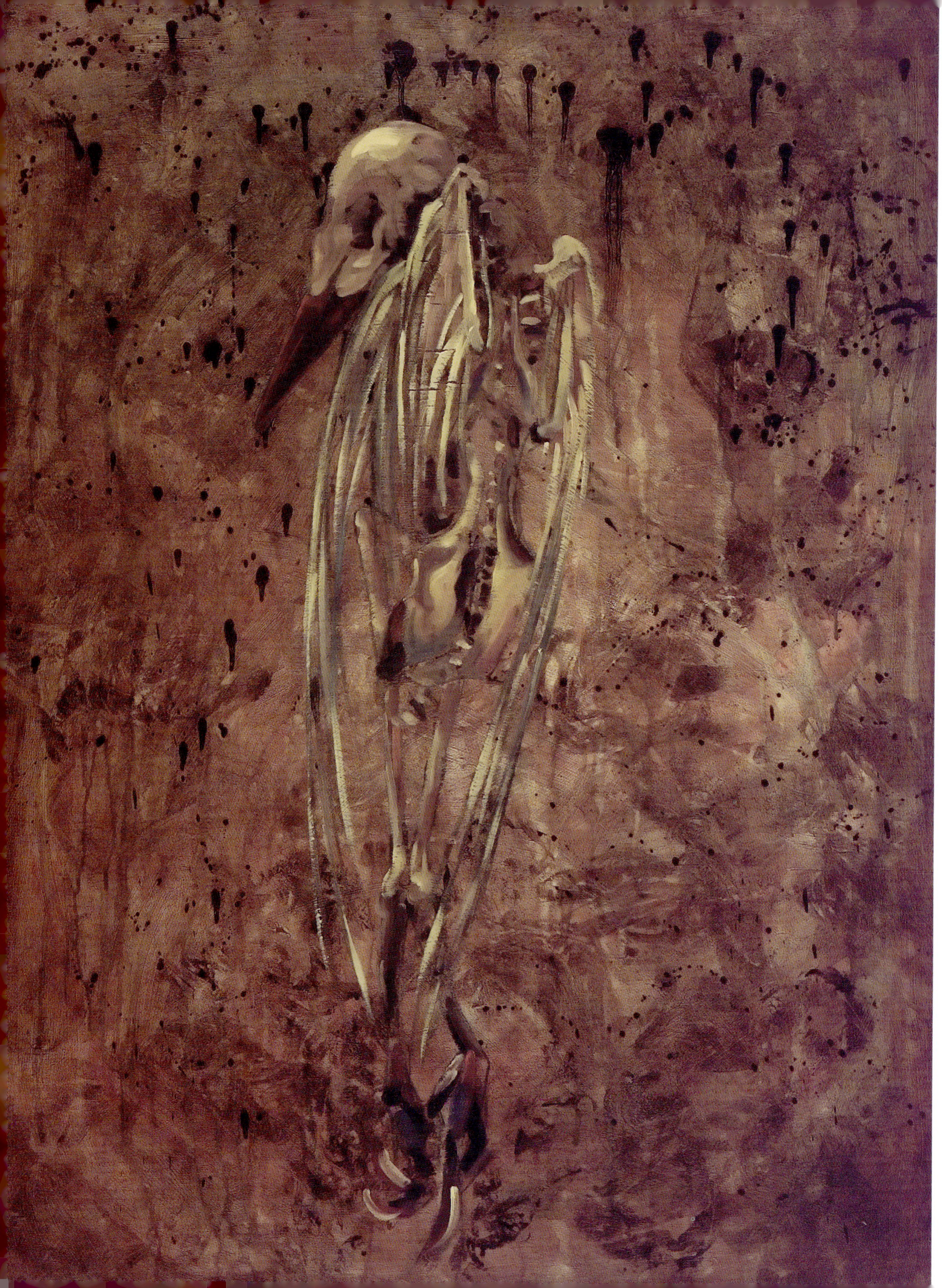

DIRECTOR'S PREFACE

Over the last fifteen years Brown's dedication to her practice and growth as an artist has made her an important presence in Manitoba's artistic community.

Many arts organizations in this province have played a part in Brown's progress as an artist. The Art Gallery of Southwestern Manitoba (AGSM) was an early and strong advocate of her work, and helped extend her reach to Winnipeg, where she received her first solo exhibition at aceartinc. Those powerful *Tornado* paintings caught the attention of The Winnipeg Art Gallery and her *Drive-In* paintings were prominently featured in the WAG's *Manitoba Studio Series*. Ten years later the AGSM highlighted Brown's work again with a solo exhibition of *The Ancient Ones* paintings, which were the beginnings of her recent *Vestiges* project.

The expansive generosity that imbues Brown's work is the same spirit that marks the mentorship she provides to developing artists. An important influence for both the southwestern Manitoba and Winnipeg artistic communities, I am delighted that our two organizations have come together to produce and present her latest work, *Vestiges*, to our respective audiences. On behalf of both organizations I would like to thank Shirley Brown for her spellbinding and wickedly humorous work and the ongoing friendship we have all shared with her. I would also like to extend my appreciation to Cathy Mattes, Mary Reid, and the staff of each gallery for lending their expertise to see this project come to fruition.

On behalf of the Art Gallery of Southwestern Manitoba and The Winnipeg Art Gallery, I would like to express our gratitude to the W.H. & S.E. Loewen Foundation for sponsoring this exhibition. I would also like to acknowledge the ongoing support provided to both institutions by the Canada Council for the Arts. The Art Gallery of Southwestern Manitoba is particularly grateful for the continued support of the Manitoba Arts Council.

Jennifer Woodbury
Director
Art Gallery of Southwestern Manitoba

Cat. 48 *Untitled #5 (Shrugger)* 2000

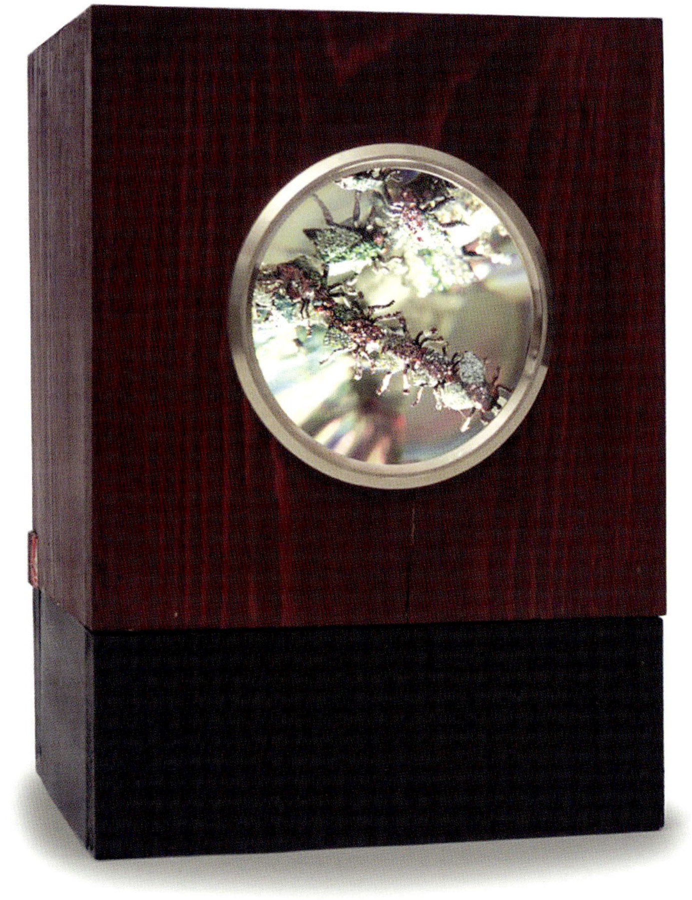

Cat. 2 *Untitled, Box #2* 2004

ARTIST STATEMENT

In 1996 I discovered a cache of 29 bird skeletons in an old cookstove. Years ago, these birds had mistakenly flown down the chimney and into the old stove where they perished. The bones were beautiful and mysterious.

I created paintings, drawings, and photographs of the skeletons. As I did this, I began to picture these poignant creatures as ancient beings from a lost civilization and, in my mind, a metaphor for loss. I decided that I would create an imagined culture in which they may have lived. To this end, I produced multimedia artifacts using the bird imagery as a source. These invented remnants of a lost world might have been uncovered by archaeologists as they investigated the newly discovered ancient society. To me, the relics are symbolic fragments of a vanished world and a lost wisdom.

I enjoy the idea of them being displayed as in a museum. There was a dignity and worth to the lives of these birds. Through this work I wanted to create a place for us to contemplate our own lives. Can we recognize anything about ourselves in the remnants of this invented world?

This body of work has allowed me to examine the essence of my fascination with unexpected disaster.

As I worked on the artifacts, I began to think about how museums often present work.

I see an irony in the manner in which today's society presents historical objects. The work is shown with reverence to denote its importance. The visitors are then funnelled through a gift shop where they are confronted with the "important" images on t-shirts and mugs.

I relish playing with the idea of commercialism and our need to remember the event with some tawdry memento. I realize that I am lured by and complicit in this mad consumerism.

This section of the exhibit allows me to play with the black humour I so enjoy.

Shirley Brown, 2005

VESTIGES

CATHY MATTES

VESTIGES

Vestige – a trace or piece of evidence; a sign

Vestiges exposes Shirley Brown's recent contemplation about the precarious nature of life. By paying homage to 29 bird skeletons she found almost ten years ago in an old cookstove on her abandoned family homestead, Brown continues her fascination with unexpected disasters – a recurring theme in her art. She searches for meaning in the birds' lives and unfortunate demise, while attempting to control the uncontrollable.

For Brown, the bones of the birds are mysterious yet vulnerable. She surmises they had mistakenly flown down the cookstove chimney and ponders the secrets they carried with them of their lives and deaths. Brown began to picture the creatures as ancient beings that may have inhabited this Earth long ago – part of a past civilization. "Artifacts" for her imagined lost society were produced, similar to those found in a cultural museum. Exploring a variety of media, including image and emulsion transfers, collage, and encaustic, she created bookworks, paintings, reliquaries, and shrines – symbolic fragments of an imagined vanished world and lost wisdom.

Brown's practice of exhibiting and creating artifacts for a lost civilization mimics museum practices of displaying cultures. According to James Clifford, "Museums create the illusion of adequate representation of a world by first cutting objects out of specific contexts and making them stand for abstract wholes."[1] A world of value is thus created. Anthropologists, historians, and curators decide what cultures are worthy of public presentation. They choose which objects should be collected, preserved, exhibited, and valued. Collections are then labelled, codified, explained, infused with interesting anecdotes, and presented according to museum or gallery standards.

Those deciding what is of value, and how to put meaning to it, have a history of fabricating through their own work the societies they purport to be discovering. Whole narratives are often presented in cultural institutions as being unbiased and factual, when they are actually fused with personal interest, experiences, motives, cultural background, and imagination.

In the eighties, anthropologist Michael M. Ames acknowledged the ways in which cultural researchers created the cultures that were their focus. According to Ames, "Anthropologists have always been in the business of reconstructing by means of their own theoretical categories the social constructions of those they study."[2] This involves reconstructing the meanings of cultural practice, historic events, and art.

It is here that Brown's process reflects some museum and gallery practices. She explored the life and death of the birds and their society in two phases. First, she photographed, made drawings of, and painted the skeletons. She studied her subjects and recorded their existence. She then created an imaginary world for them through her creation and collection of artifacts.

However, unlike anthropologists, Brown does not present her lost bird civilization as proof of certain truths. They are hints of what may have been, and overtly reveal her imagination, wants, own experiences, and views of the world. Brown does not present a linear narrative about the creatures, as is often found in museums. Nor does she provide labels, didactics, or codes that explain the material objects. Instead she invites viewers to create their own fragmented narrative about the creatures based on their own imagination, wants, and experiences.

Brown's search for meaning in fantasy civilizations mirrors science fiction, in particular the famous series *Star Trek*. In the series, the Federation is an organization of various alien societies. Sometimes alien races from the Federation are in conflict with the Starship Enterprise, and other times rely on the officers to aid them in their time of need. The alien societies often mirror the human race, and almost always have their own religious beliefs, language, wars, art, and culture. Often, the alien life forms are superior to the humans onboard the Enterprise and, in many ways, have wisdom that the human race does not yet hold. It is within this familiar fantasy premise that viewers can locate Brown's art.

The artifacts in *Vestiges* contain aspects that could be attributed to human societies, but instead represent a potential bird civilization. Many of Brown's artifacts are housed in this untitled series of 36 wooden boxes. The boxes open to an attached light box that illuminates the interior. Viewers look into the boxes through a convex lens to find the artifacts. The contained artifacts imply the birds had their own creation stories, music, language, scientific beliefs, enemies (the armoured bugs), and ideals of beauty. The specifics of these things that constitute societies are very ambiguous, but the boxes allude to their existence. The convex lens that magnifies and transforms the interior is indicative of how humans can interpret meaning and locate the self within.

Game Box suggests a favourite pastime for the birds. It contains a rectangular wooden box with clay squares that have various symbols ingrained on them. Reminiscent of checkers and chess, *Game Box* is familiar yet inexplicable. Many of us have taken part in playing board games as a form of recreation and understand their purpose. However, within the display of *Game Box* there are no explanations of the significance of the game, or how and when the game would have been played. We as viewers are thus left to our own devices to search for understanding, and to imagine how the birds played the game.

Included in the exhibition are photo albums that contain visual hints of the faith systems of the bird society. Reminiscent of a bible, they appear to hold all our answers to the bird society, but we cannot decode its content. Depending on our own belief system, we interpret what the bible meant to the bird society. The bible taunts viewers because it does not supply definite answers to our questions, which museum exhibitions usually purport to provide.

Brown's other artifacts continue to stir feelings of loss and mystery. *Ossuary 1 & 2* contain actual bird skeletons placed as if in a shrine, evoking melancholy about their demise and the unanswered questions we have about them. These tomb boxes are reminiscent of an exhibition of King Tutankhamun's treasures that travelled around the world in the eighties. Presented in this exhibition were material objects that hinted at how ancient societies existed, including tomb boxes that contained a mummified King Tut.

Located in *Community Box* are small, decorated rectangular boxes. These contain found objects given to Brown for a community art project in 2002 when she asked peers to create art works with the rectangular boxes. This piece most openly fuses her reality and fantasy; however, the display of the boxes – some open but most tied shut – evokes secrecy and, similar to the ossuary, melancholy.

There are five paintings in the exhibition featuring bird skeletons. While studying the birds, Brown gave them nicknames based on their form: *Red Beak*, *Picker*, *Flinger*, *Knuckle Dragger*, and *Shrugger*. The paintings of these characters expose Brown's study process and

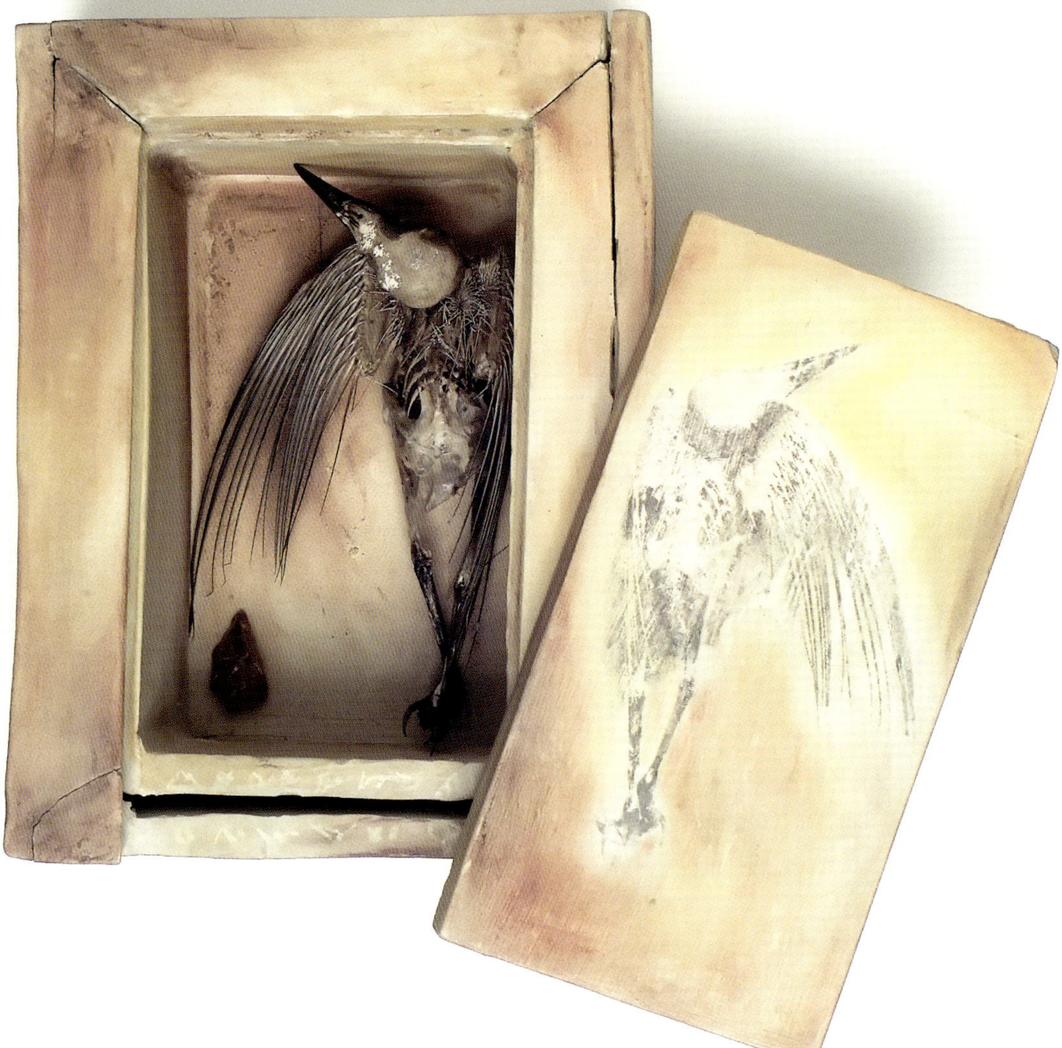

Cat. 42 *Ossuary #1* 2004-05

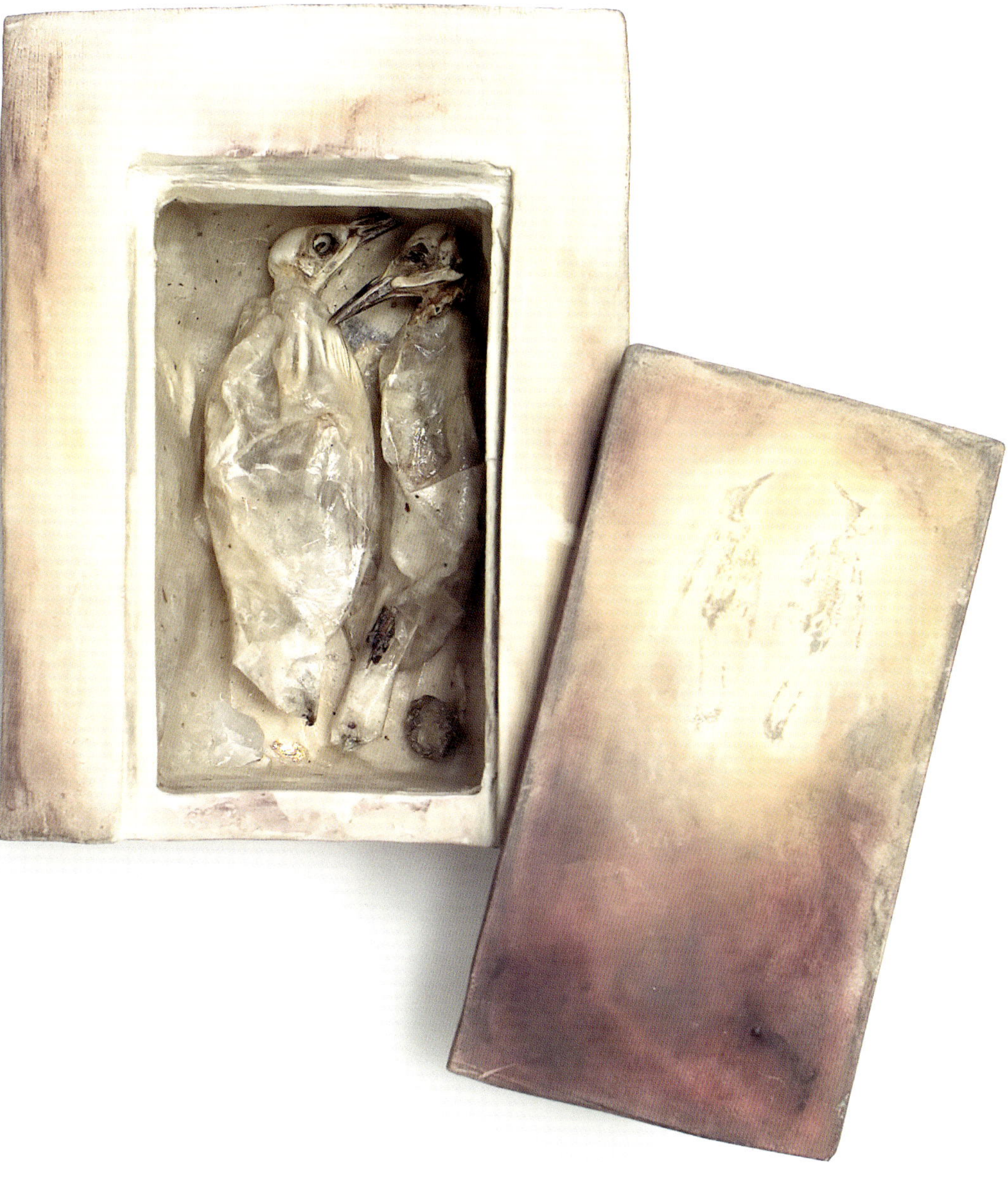

Cat. 43 *Ossuary #2* 2004-05

how she applied personalities to the birds – humanized them. The paintings of the birds are reminiscent of historic paintings of important figures that may be included in historic museum exhibitions. They are points of departure to examine the creatures' societies and give personality and purpose to their existence and end.

Playing with ideas of consumerism, Brown has devoted a portion of the exhibition to a faux gift shop that contains trite mementos such as t-shirts, mugs, and magnets with images of the bird skeletons. These items are not for sale. This is in response to the ironic manner in which museums and galleries present important historical art, or important histories, and then funnel viewers into gift shops where they can purchase souvenirs as a means to remember the exhibitions. Brown's faux gift shop raises questions about how traditional gift shops devalue the experience of museum and gallery visitors.

Gift shops are often geared toward the cultural tourist, who is more interested in having 'been there' and recording their experience through purchasing mementos as opposed to having some kind of profound experience when engaging with museum exhibitions.[3] With the gift shop component Brown is asking: How conditioned are visitors to expect such a shop? Do we not trust ourselves to remember the event or feeling we experienced without a souvenir? Will they react when the gimmick of seduction is denied? Will the gallery visitors question their desire to buy? The humourous nature of the gift shop, complete with the museum-like exhibition display, raises questions about how civilizations are presented/fabricated in museums and galleries, and how consumerism is involved in museum and gallery practices.

Brown's work is an exercise in making the world her own. She searches for understanding of her own reality by looking to the lost bird civilization. The invented relics Brown creates for these creatures are a metaphor for both personal and societal loss, and raise the questions: What is worthy of remembrance in our own lives? Can we recognize anything about ourselves in the remnants of the creatures' invented world?

NOTES

1. James Clifford, "On Collecting Art and Culture," in *Out There: Marginalization and Contemporary Cultures* (The New Museum of Contemporary Art, MIT Press, 1990) p.144.

2. Michael M. Ames, "How Anthropologists Help to Fabricate the Cultures They Study" in *Museums, The Public and Anthropology – A Study in the Anthropology of Anthropology (University of British Columbia Press and Concept Publishing Company, Vancouver and New Delhi: 1986)* p.58.

3. Joan Acland, *The Native Artistic Subject and National Identity: A Cultural Analysis of the Architecture of the Canadian Museum of Civilization, Designed by Douglas J. Cardinal* (Concordia University, Montreal, PhD Thesis, 1994), p.41.

Cat. 51 *Gift Shop Installation* (detail) 2005

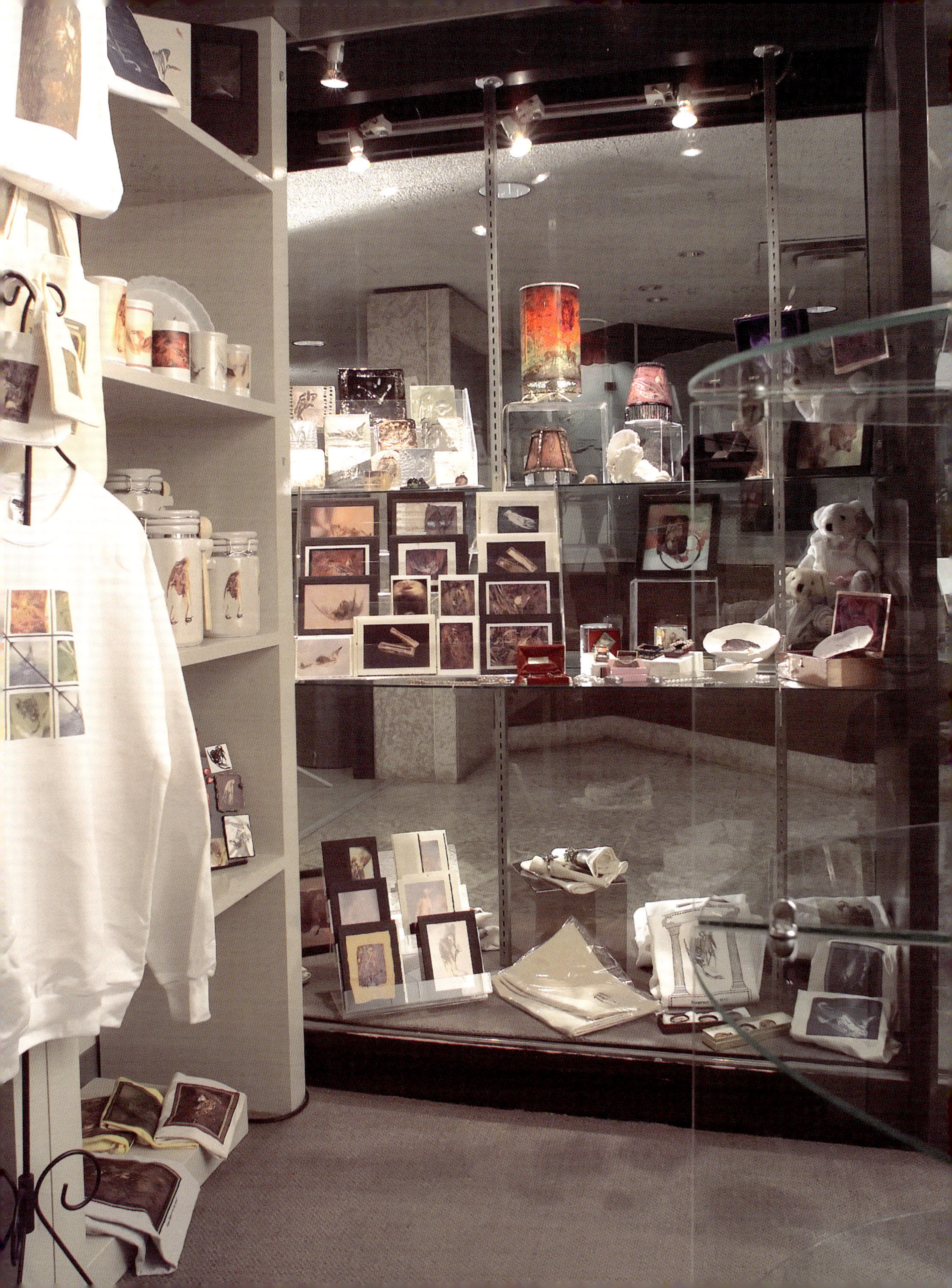

THE LAND OF FLICKERY

MARY REID

THE LAND OF FLICKERY

As told to Mary Reid by art(hropolog)ist Shirley Brown

A long time ago in the enchanted Land of Flickery there lived a little flicker called Picker. He was a scrawny little bird who was often teased by his much bigger hatch mates. Perhaps because of this, he grew up shy and socially inept, preferring solitude to the company of others.

To the undiscerning eye most flickers looked identical, but each bird was born with a unique characteristic. Picker's unique characteristic became his unfortunate name, chosen by the elders and given to him during the lavish naming ceremony. Although Picker did not understand it at the time, this characteristic would ultimately be his legacy.

• • • • • • • • • • • •

Flickery was known far and wide for its ritualized games and elaborate tournaments. The complex amusement used ancient clay tiles passed down through many generations and believed to be as powerful as the player who handled them. At times the fate of the winner had as much to do with the skills of the players as it did with the mystical power of the ceramic pieces themselves.

When it came to picking a team for the tournament, Picker was always the last to be selected. And instead of being chosen by his peers, he was usually placed in a group by his tutor, which provoked snips of disapproval from those he had been foisted upon. He didn't do well in the games and preferred to stand to the side, quietly picking away with his teeny beak.

One day Picker noticed something the other flickers did not. They were only interested in the placement of their individual pieces and advancing their position in the game. He, however, observed that certain tiles interacted when in close proximity to or a great distance from one another, and that prints and designs on the tiles magically and magnetically aligned with or repelled others. He also felt the undercurrent of vibrating energy within the ceramic squares, and heard a small high-pitched noise when certain patterns appeared.

Was a larger symbol created when the tiles were in a certain order? If so, what did it mean? And why had no one thought of this or tried it before? Did it have anything to do with the way the tiles were stored, each in their own compartment, in a random order? Picker decided it best to keep his suspicions to himself for the time being, and life by the sidelines continued along as usual.

Soon, however, things changed for Picker when he began learning about the importance of the clear quartz crystals in Flickery's long honoured religion. Throughout the ages, all flickers paid homage to the quartz crystals, which were believed to have a special power that brought prosperity, love, and respect.

While learning about the crystals, Picker wondered if there was a connection to the gaming tiles. He decided to conduct his own research at the great Flicker Library, a most regal and formidable place and one of the oldest buildings in all the land. The library's impressive holding was so large that some books were overlooked, left to languish in unread darkness. It was in these that Picker hoped to find answers to his questions.

Picker roamed the stacks of the great library, looking for a connection between the crystal religion and gaming. His unassuming presence meant he was often forgotten when the elders locked up for the night, which suited him just fine since he was then free to fly from shelf to shelf undisturbed.

The reading was daunting and unfruitful until one night Picker came across a locked chamber in the library, which he rightly assumed held the most rare and sacred books of Flickery. Rather than risk drawing attention to himself, he waited until after the library had closed before using his particularly dexterous beak to pick the lock and gain entry into this hallowed part of the library.

Once inside, Picker found an ornate collection of ancient flicker crystal bibles. It was in one particular bible that he noticed images of the gaming pieces running along the inside cover. The clay tiles were illustrated in a specific order that fashioned a code – a code that, once broken, foretold a future too horrifying to think of, a truth so terrible that Picker was

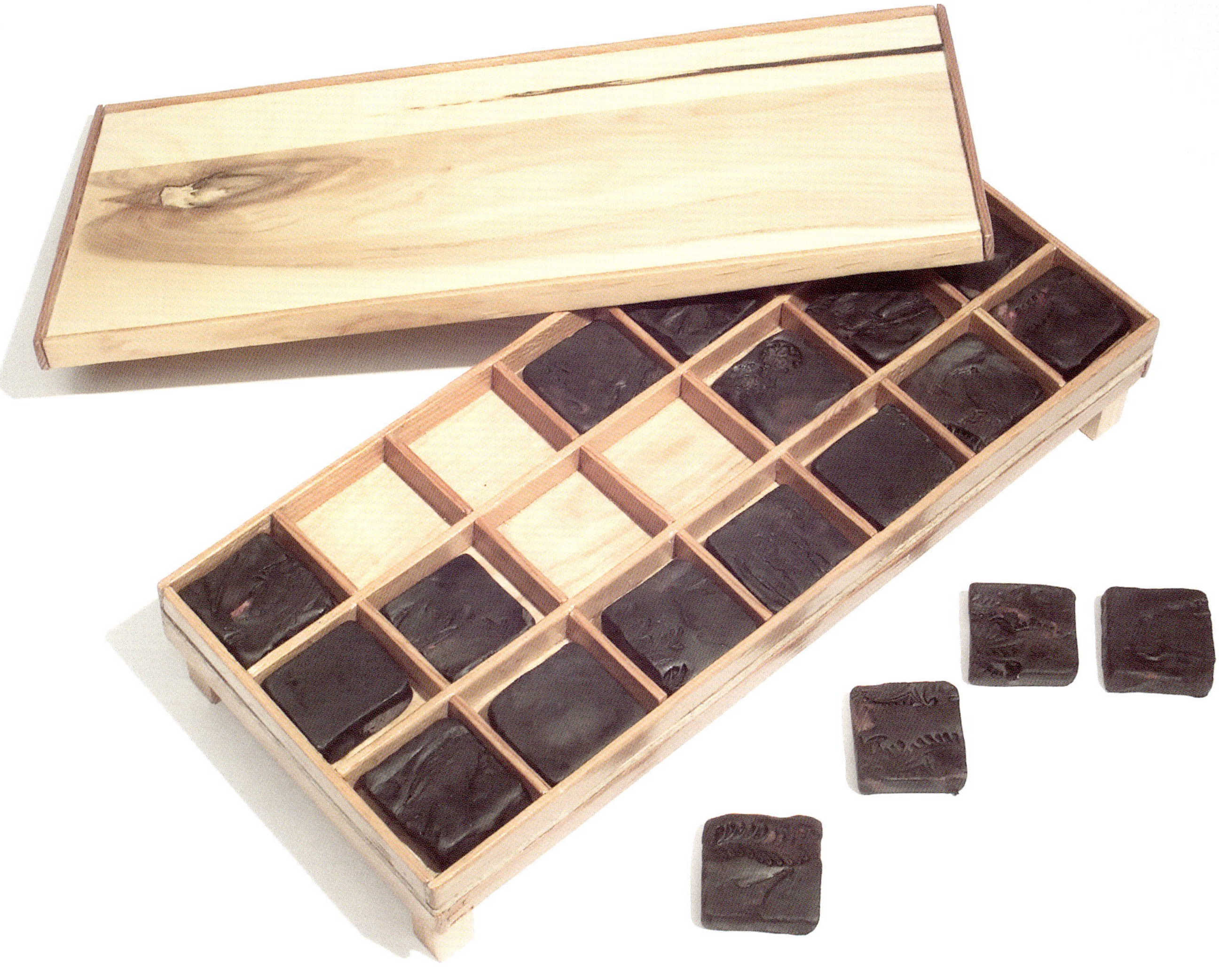

Cat. 38 *Game Box* 2003

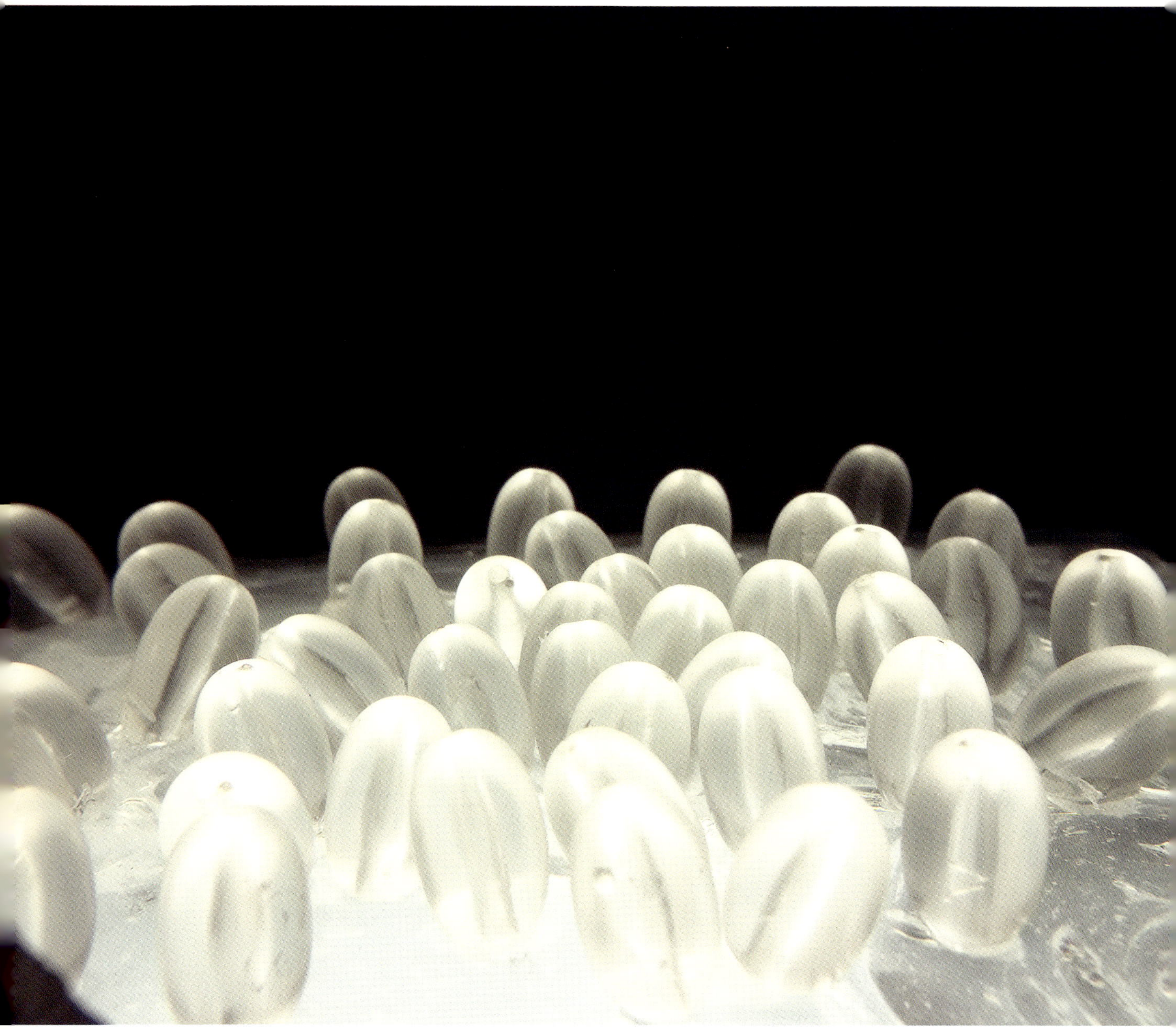

Cat. 19 *Untitled, Box #19* (detail) 2003

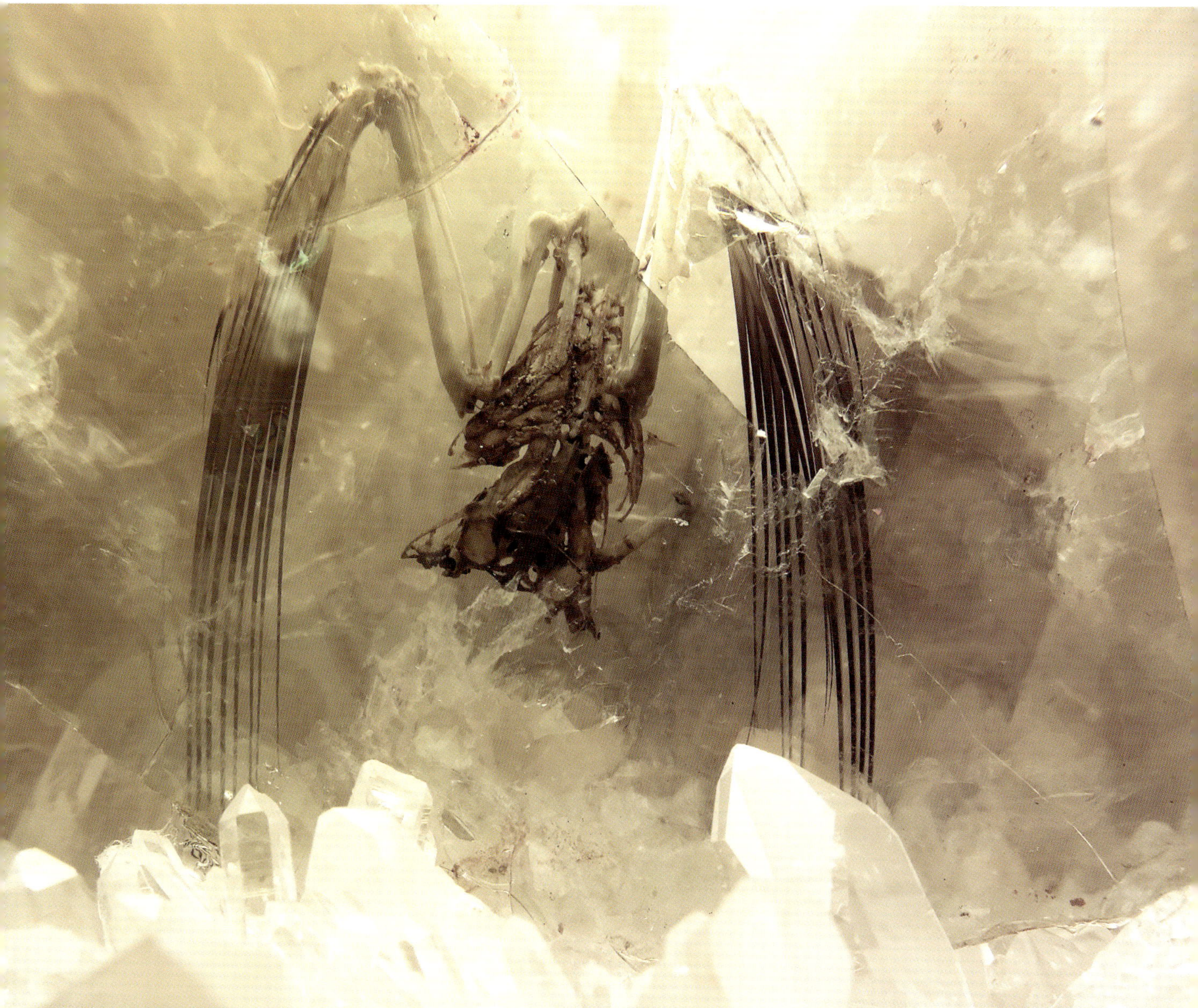

Cat. 3 *Untitled, Box #3* (detail) 2004

sure no one would believe him.

The next morning Picker awoke to some dreadful news – that Flickery's most precious and powerful crystal, the crystal of ALL crystals, the Great Crystal, had been stolen from its sacred sanctuary. This was incredible news since this holiest of holy place was located down in the deepest and darkest part of a large cavern. The guardian flickers had met an unspeakable fate and Flickery's future looked bleak. You see, not only was the crystal an object of worship, but for as long as any flicker could remember, it also provided all life-supporting power for the entire land. Without its energy, life for flickers would change drastically, bringing disease and unrest to their idyllic land. The power supply surplus had already been depleted, with only a limited amount of stored power left to live off.

As was the custom in Flickery, flickers graduating from the highest level of branch instruction were required to embark on a great quest to complete their studies. That day Picker learned that his classmates were being sent to recover the stolen crystal. He raised his little claw to object but it was too late. Flocks were already being formed, maps drawn out, plans hatched – there was no time to waste. As usual, Picker was not included in any of the search parties, and no one noticed when he quietly flew off on his own.

With his classmates off in search of the great crystal, Picker returned to the library. He waited in the stacks until the elders had moved to another room, and as he had done before, picked the lock of the sacred library chamber. He quickly retrieved the ancient crystal bible that contained the gaming pieces symbols, and swiftly ripped out the part he wanted.

Grasping the pages safely in his beak, Picker flew as fast as he could to the room where the most precious gaming tiles were kept. He easily picked that lock as well, which momentarily caused him to grin with pride at his new skill, almost dropping the precious text in the process! Once inside the small room, Picker unrolled the paper and studied it closely. He realized that he could not lay out the tiles in the necessary configuration in this space and knew there was only one place to do this – the Great Crystal Sanctuary.

The tiles were heavy and Picker could only handle one at a time. Still, one by one he brought each clay gaming tile into the Sanctuary. At first he was careful not to disturb the elders who were there investigating the crime, but soon realized that they were too preoccupied to even notice him, let alone care about what he was doing.

Finally, all the tiles were deep inside the cavern and Picker carefully placed them in the order outlined on the bible page. With each consecutive placement, the pieces began to vibrate and hum, until the tone was so high that it was almost deafening. He could not explain it but Picker felt stronger and more confident than ever before. When all the ceramic squares were together, the whole puzzle emanated a glowing red-hot light and Picker read out loud the code that had formed:

flickers and flies, are fathered by one, to forget this is the fate of one and the folly of the other, fear flies, fear fire, fear failure

Suddenly the tiles burst into flame, instantly re-establishing the power supply with the energy from the heat and returning the Land of Flickery to full power. Flickers all over squawked in delight. Little did they know that Picker had sadly perished in the fire, as did twenty-eight flicker elders who had flown down the dark cavern to investigate what was going on.

Gone but no longer forgotten, Picker was renamed Red Beak – a more ceremonious name – by the other flickers when they celebrated his life during the next gaming tournament. He went down in history as the flicker who saved his fellow flickers from possible extinction, and his remains, along with those of the elders, were left to guard the great clay fire for all eternity.

Meanwhile, still on their fateful quest, Picker's … that is … Red Beak's classmates discovered that the neighbouring faction of flies had stolen the great crystal. There had long been resentment from the flies toward the birds, with flies nothing more than a food source for flickers, but what had unknowingly begun was a gruesome war between the two groups that would last for many generations and ultimately lead to the destruction of the Land of Flickery.

Did the flies bring the downfall of the flickers? Did the flickers do it to themselves? Are flies and flickers in fact distant cousins? These and other questions would stay unanswered for a very long time.

Until 1996 when feisty art(hropolog)ist Shirley Brown discovered 29 pristinely preserved specimens of this ancient bird culture. Finding a long ago vanished society filled Brown with complete yet uneasy joy, and she was hesitant about immediately sharing her find with the world. Instead, she continued to research this intriguing unknown civilization, slowly unearthing objects owned by the birds, such as books, bibles, games, and tools. Over time the skeletons of the birds and their accompanying materials began to tell Brown their story …

When the land surrounding us was still enchanted and untouched, an industrious society of flicker birds existed. During the height of their productivity, this group developed a complex system of tools, technology, and language. Undoubtedly there was a strong connection between the bird society, the materials they had available to them, and the techniques they employed. In several instances, elements of gold, copper, clay, and rare gemstones are evidenced in the ruins unearthed by Brown. Traditionally thought to be "pre-technical," flickers were in fact quite advanced and had successfully developed computerized system-types and built ornate architectural structures. They were able to achieve a certain level of abundance and leisure time through the introductions of mechanization. As with many ancient societies, the flickers' knowledge of these advanced technologies was unfortunately lost with their extinction.

The materials and wisdom gained by the birds is thought to be a consequence of the ritualistic journeys to far away lands that were taken by every young adult bird. These quests brought great prosperity and wealth, and this sense of luxury is evident in the gold and fabric employed in their decoration.

Brown was fortunate to find several reliquaries and shrines of the flickers still intact. Thought to have a complex social structure based on a personal belief system and crystal religion, their language consisted of a series of codes and symbols unreadable yet surprisingly discernible to the human mind.

In a society composed of strict codes of behaviour regarding relationships between gender and class, each flicker had remarkably similar physiognomy. Upon closer inspection, however, each displayed their own unique personality.

Through her research Brown unearthed the flickers' egg chamber. Consisting of tiny whitish eggs, the nursery evokes an otherworldly and almost cosmic entity atmosphere. A highly organized and efficient familial structure, the flicker embryos are presided over by one flicker at a time, working in shifts, thereby freeing up other female birds to carry out their destiny and continually contribute to the success and achievement of the entire species.

Baby flickers are raised communally with no sense of familial allegiances. There are no individual mothers and fathers in Flickery. Status, position, and duty of each individual flicker are assigned prior to breaking through the shell, regardless of biology. This form of extended family eliminates emotional ties, thereby freeing the mind and body for more productive pursuits.

Brown believes that flickers and flies lived in harmony, but ultimately the flies – terrible things dressed in beautiful packages of impenetrable jewelled armour – brought about the downfall of the flickers.

While maintaining the dignity, value, and worth of the lives of these birds, Brown's investigation brings forth the idea that a belief in progress is in fact a belief in an end. Did the flickers' liberation from daily toil in fact end their dream? Could the flickers foretell that their progress was in fact headed for extinction? Undoubtedly the maximization of growth is paired with nature's relentless energy to pull civilization back into the ground.

For Brown and her ancient ones, new things are being discovered every day. Great recorders of their own history, Brown has preserved her flicker evidence in magic portals that hold and display the remains of a place, and that create history in a multitude of individual, private, and public meanings. These windows are views that are not only vestiges and remembrances of a dead society, but also simultaneous gateways into the future of ruins.

"Ruins are enchanting because the function these things once fulfilled has gone off like a bird flying away from its nest. We are left with objects that have a hollowness that we can fill with our own wonder and fantasy." – Thomas Moore, *Re-enchantment of Everyday Life*

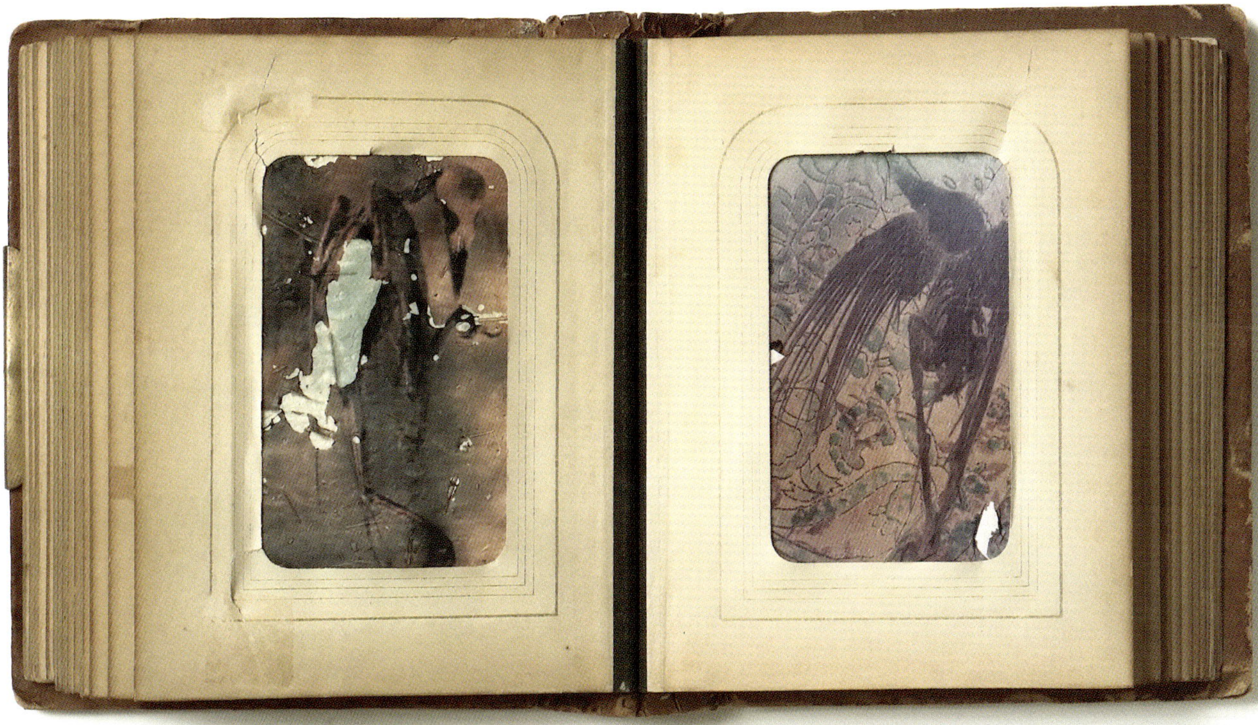

Cat. 39 *Untitled, Book #1* 2004-05

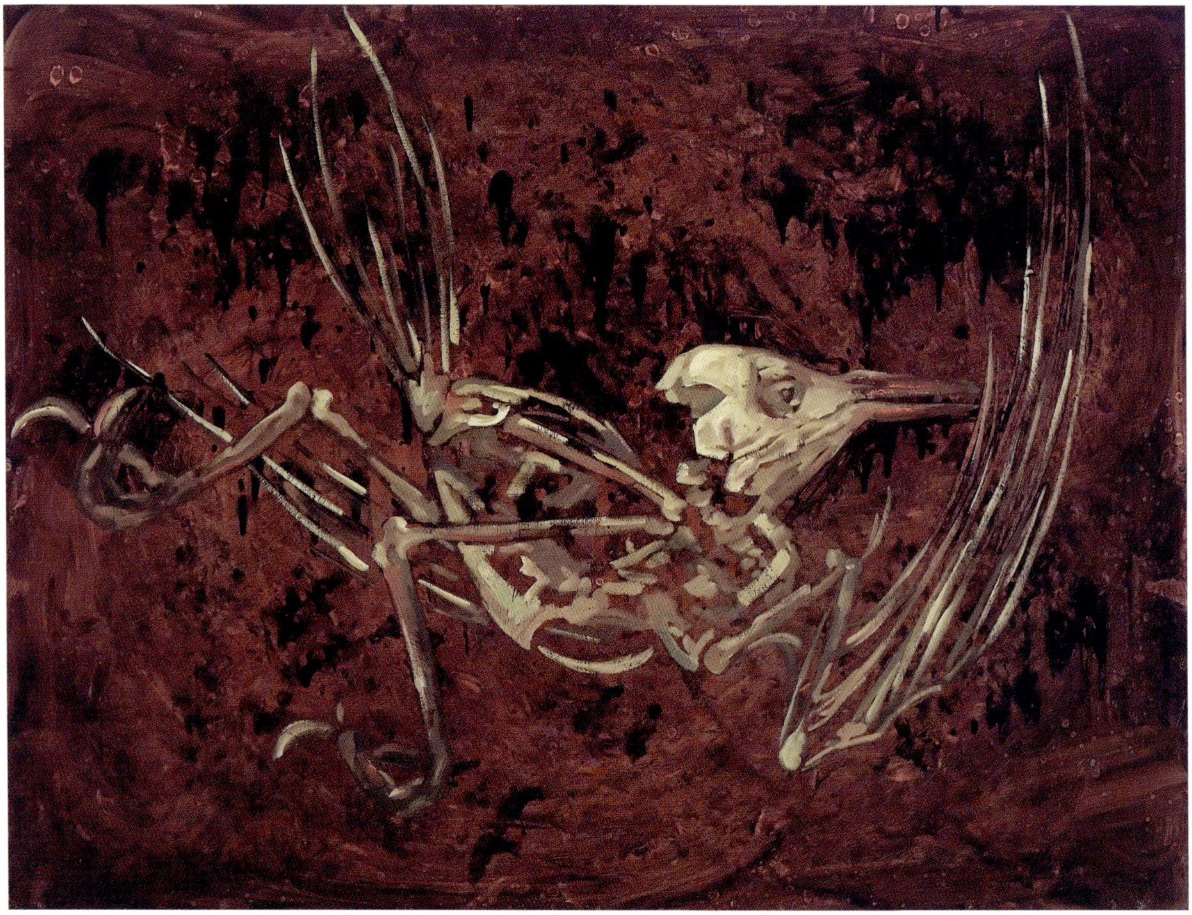

Cat. 45 *Untitled #2 (Flinger)* 2000

Cat. 46 *Untitled #3 (Picker)* 2000

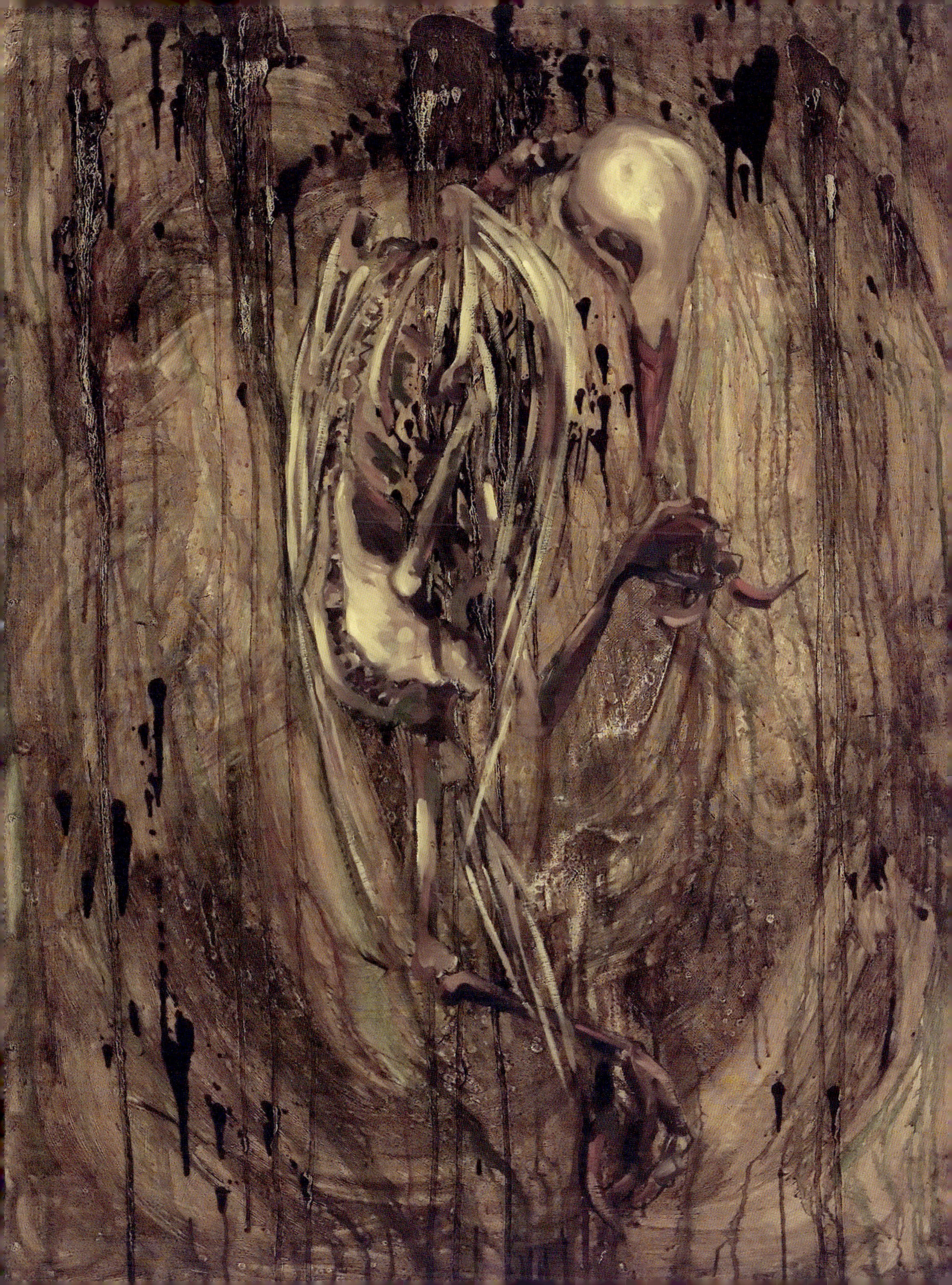

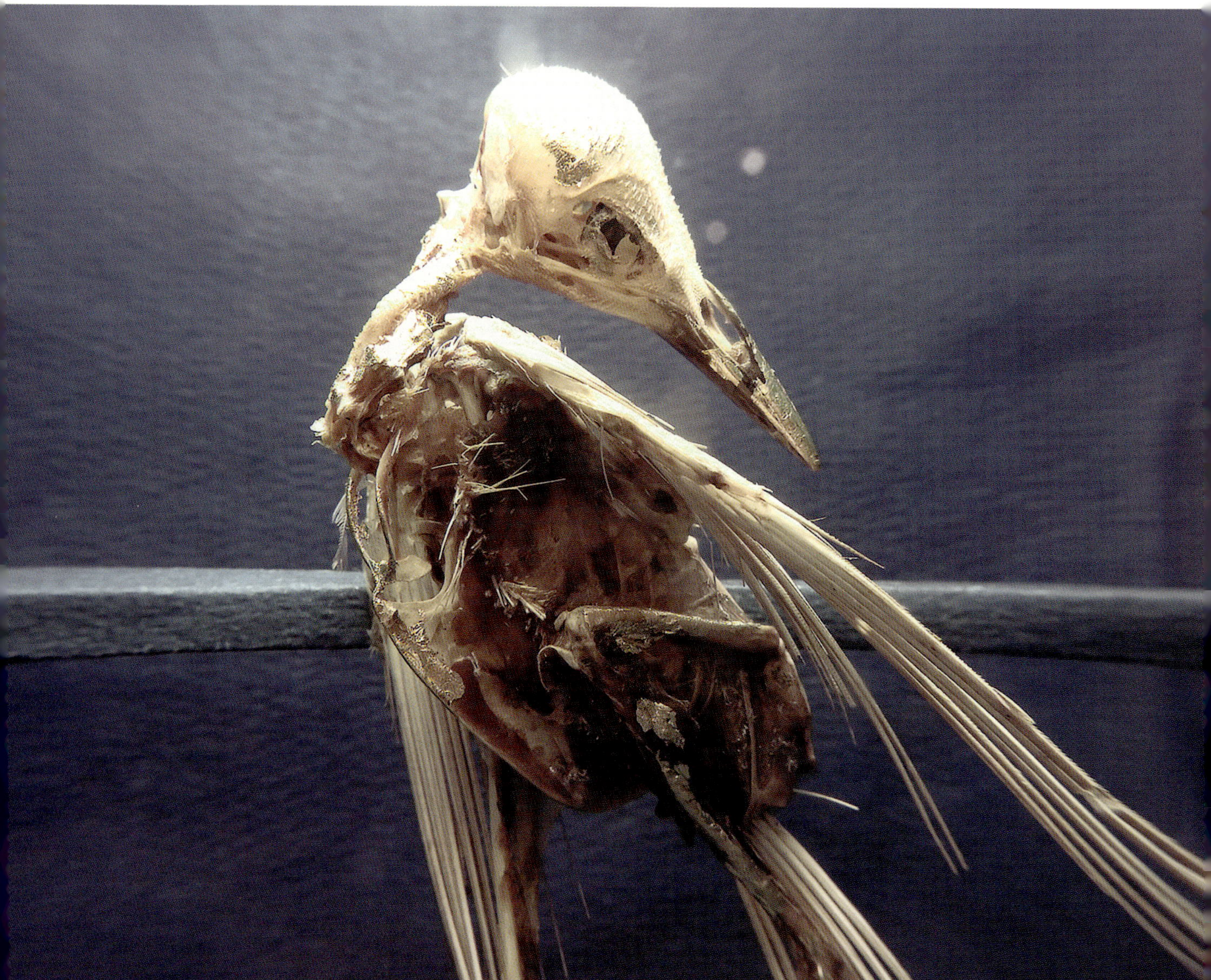

Cat. 34 *Untitled, Box #34* (detail) 2004

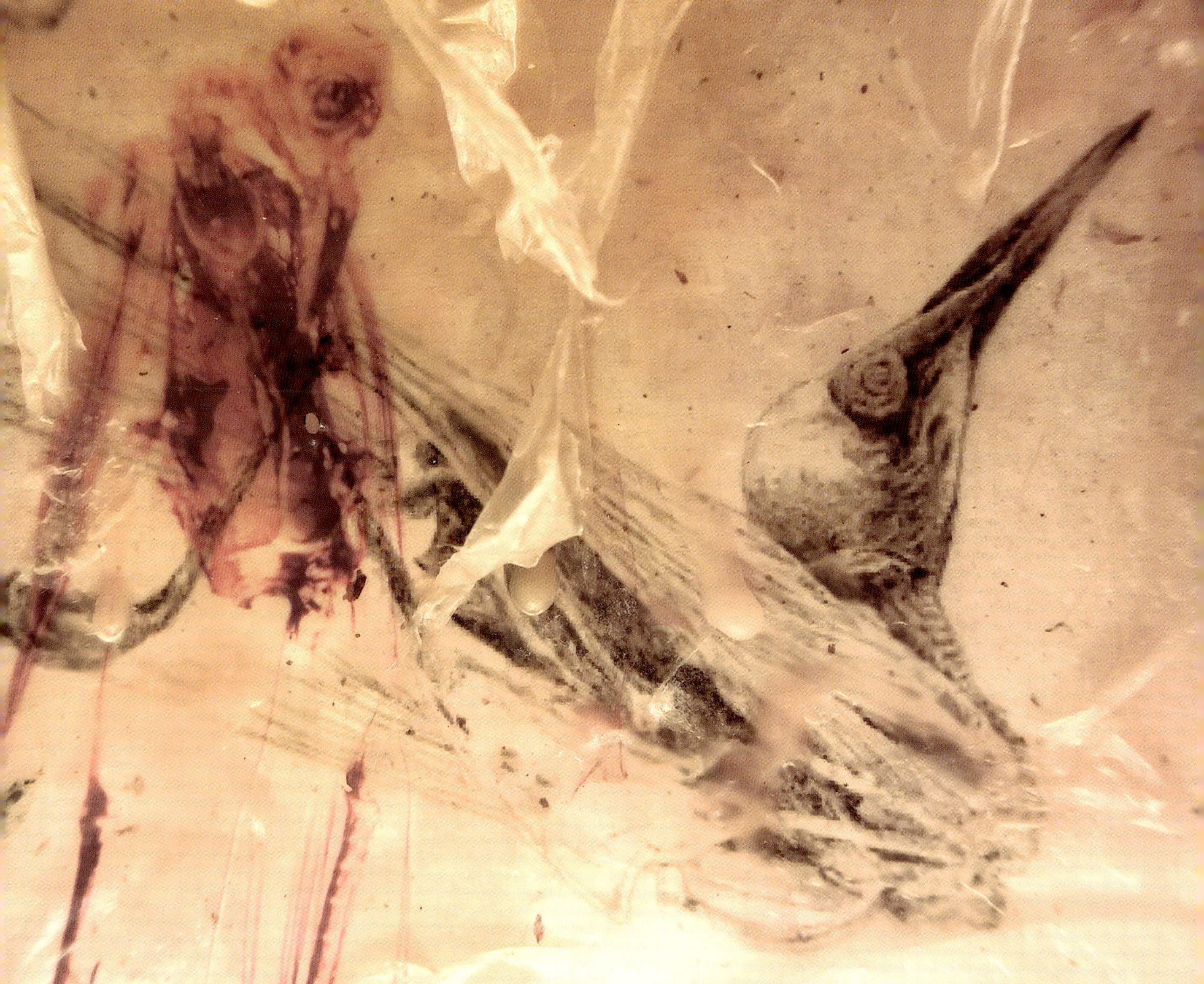

Cat. 4 *Untitled, Box #4* (detail) 2004

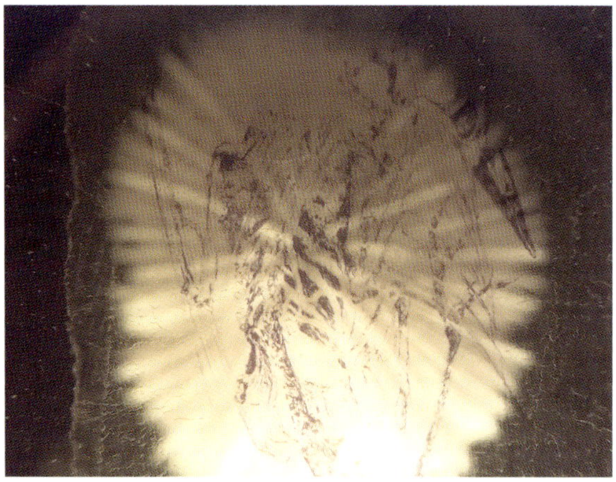

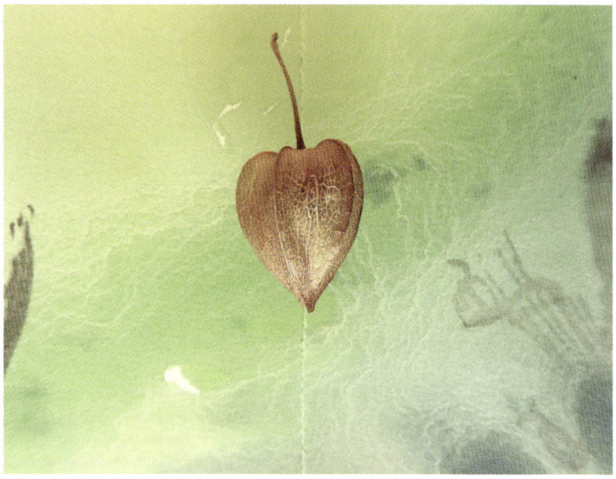

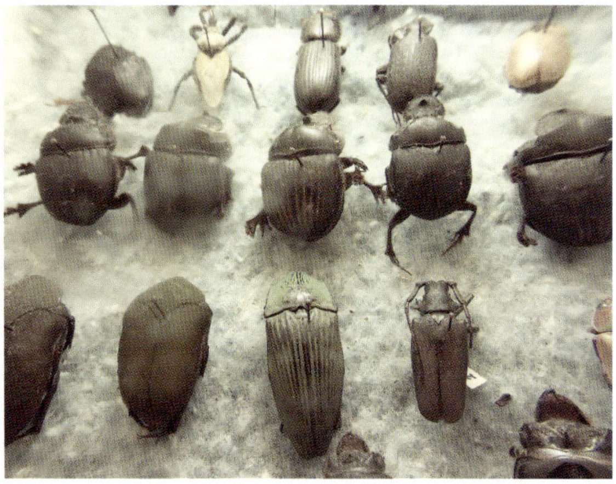

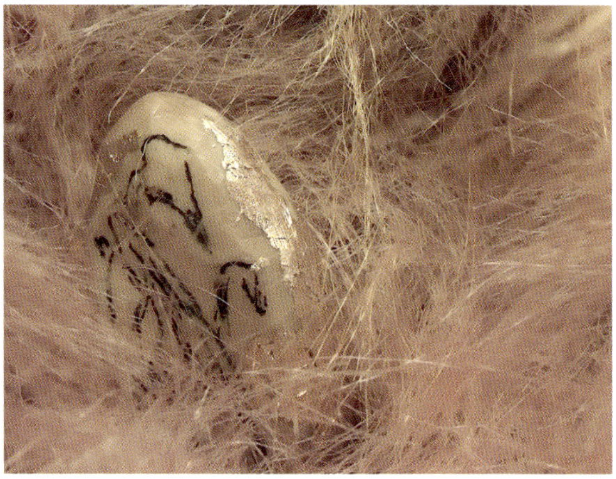

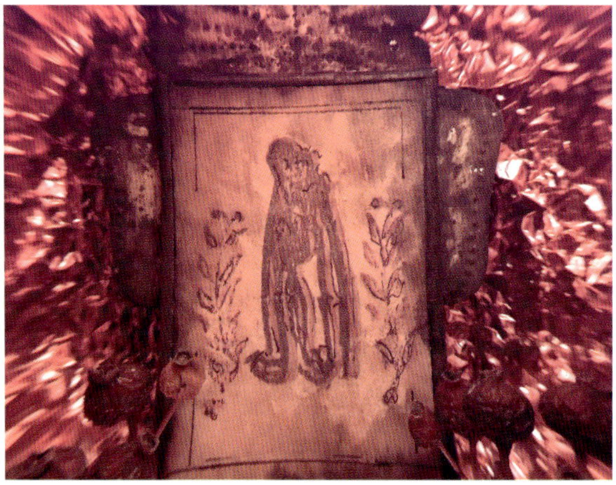

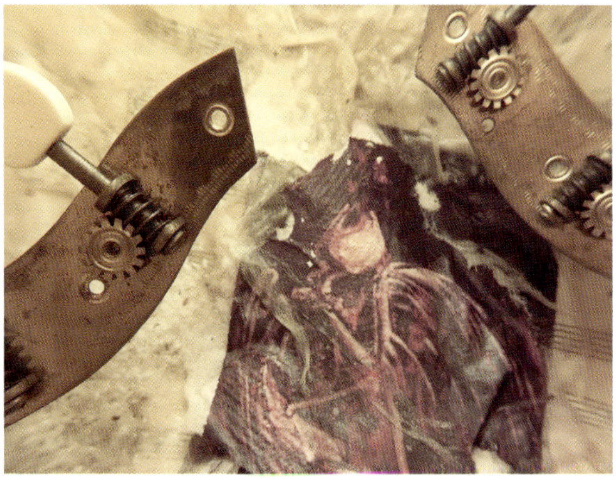

CLOCKWISE FROM TOP LEFT: Cat. 28 *Untitled, Box #28* (detail) 2004, Cat. 25 *Untitled, Box #25* (detail) 2003, Cat. 9 *Untitled, Box #9* (detail) 2003, Cat. 36 *Untitled, Box #36* (detail) 2004-05, Cat. 5 *Untitled, Box #5* (detail) 2004, Cat. 35 *Untitled, Box #35* (detail) 2004

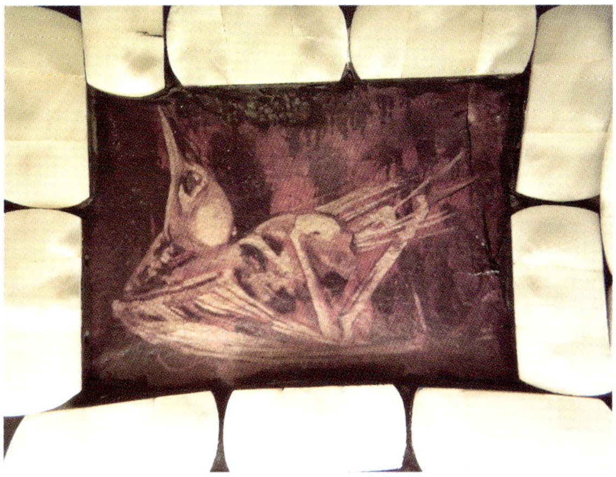
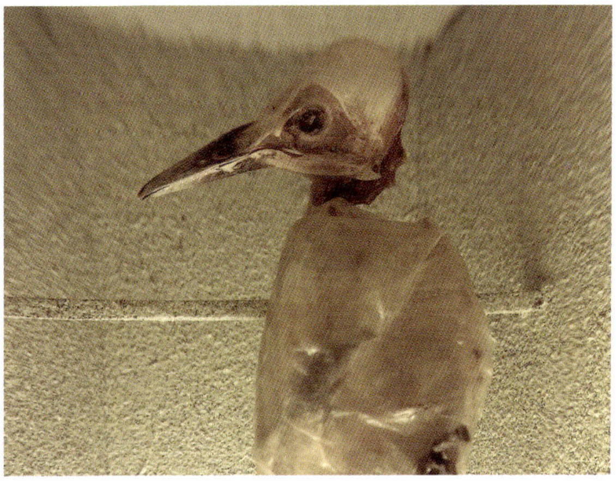
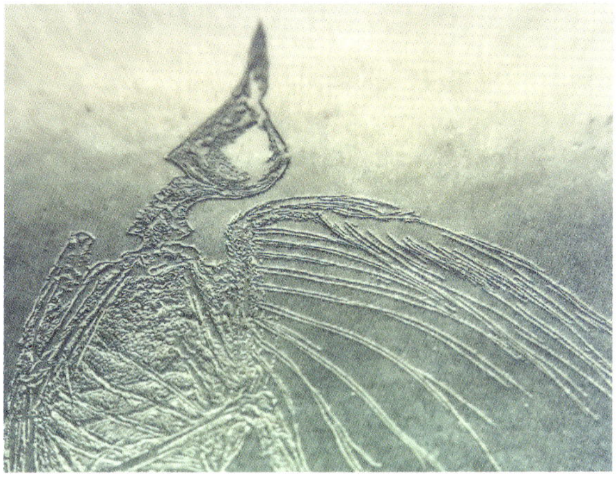
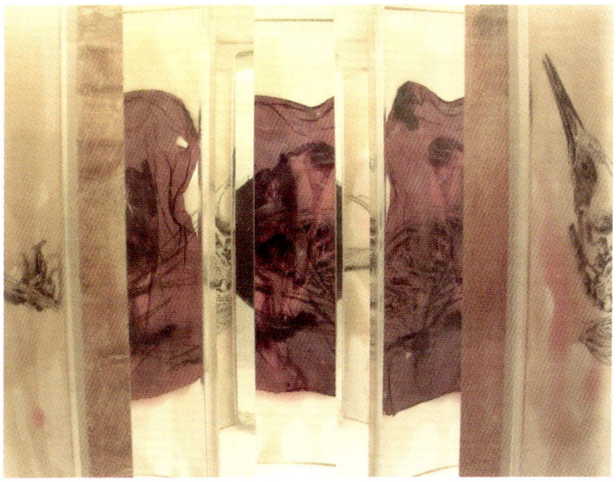
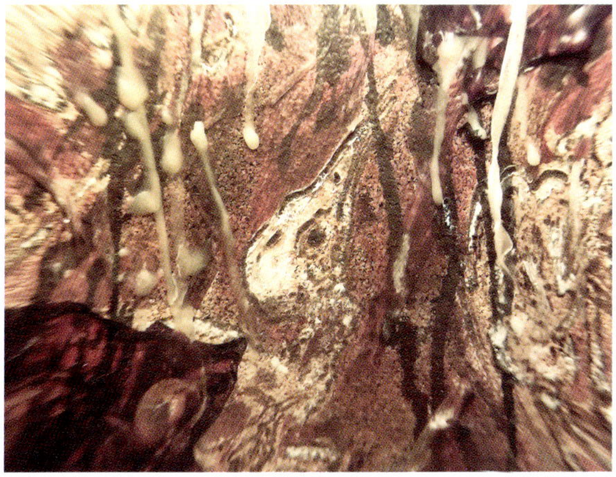
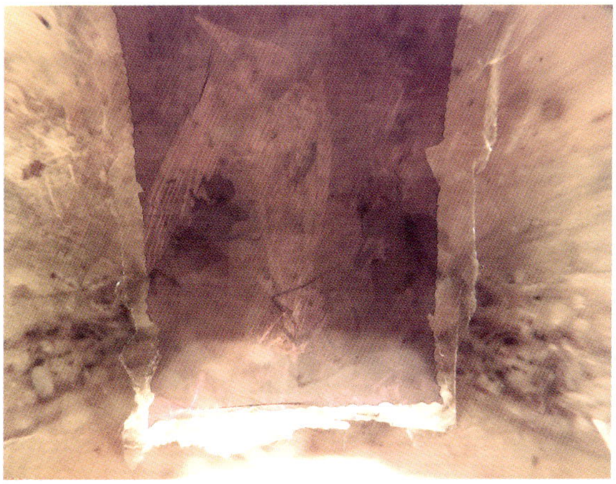

CLOCKWISE FROM TOP LEFT: Cat. 14 *Untitled, Box #14* (detail) 2004, Cat. 24 *Untitled, Box #24* (detail) 2004, Cat. 18 *Untitled, Box #18* (detail) 2004, Cat.30 *Untitled, Box #30* (detail) 2004, Cat. 23 *Untitled, Box #23* (detail) 2004, Cat. 7 *Untitled, Box #7* (detail) 2003

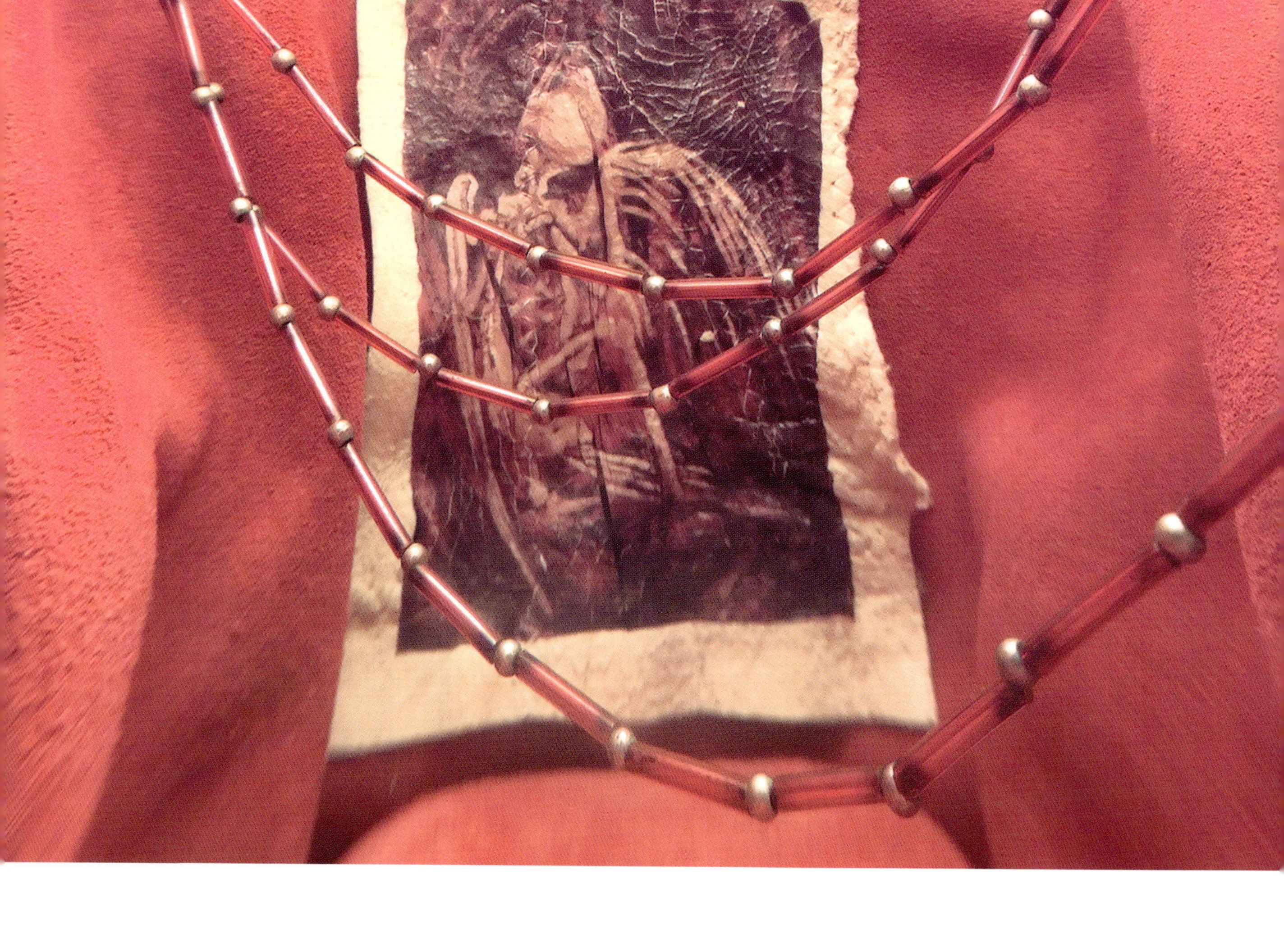

Cat. 27 *Untitled, Box #27* (detail) 2004

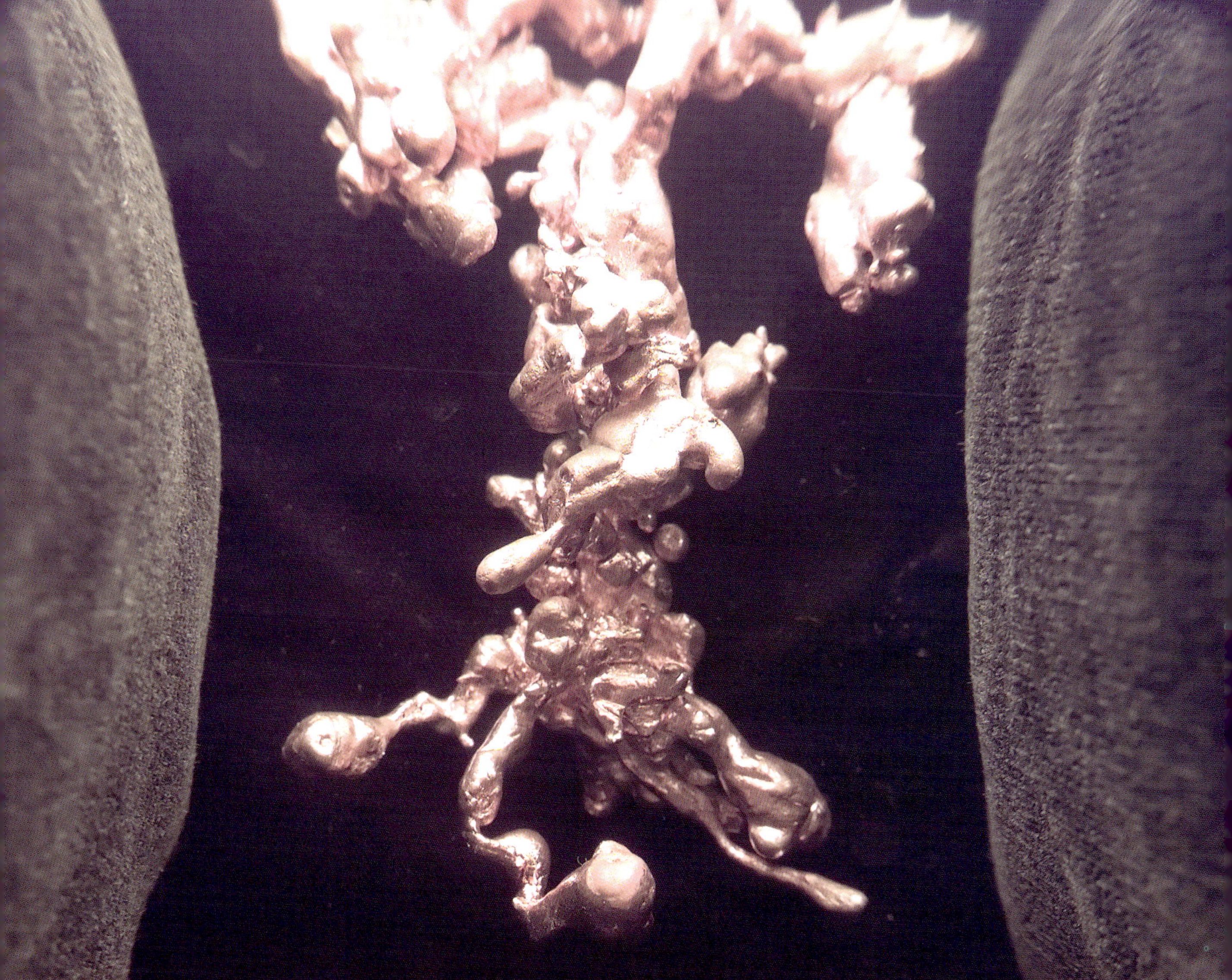

Cat. 16 *Untitled, Box #16* (detail) 2004

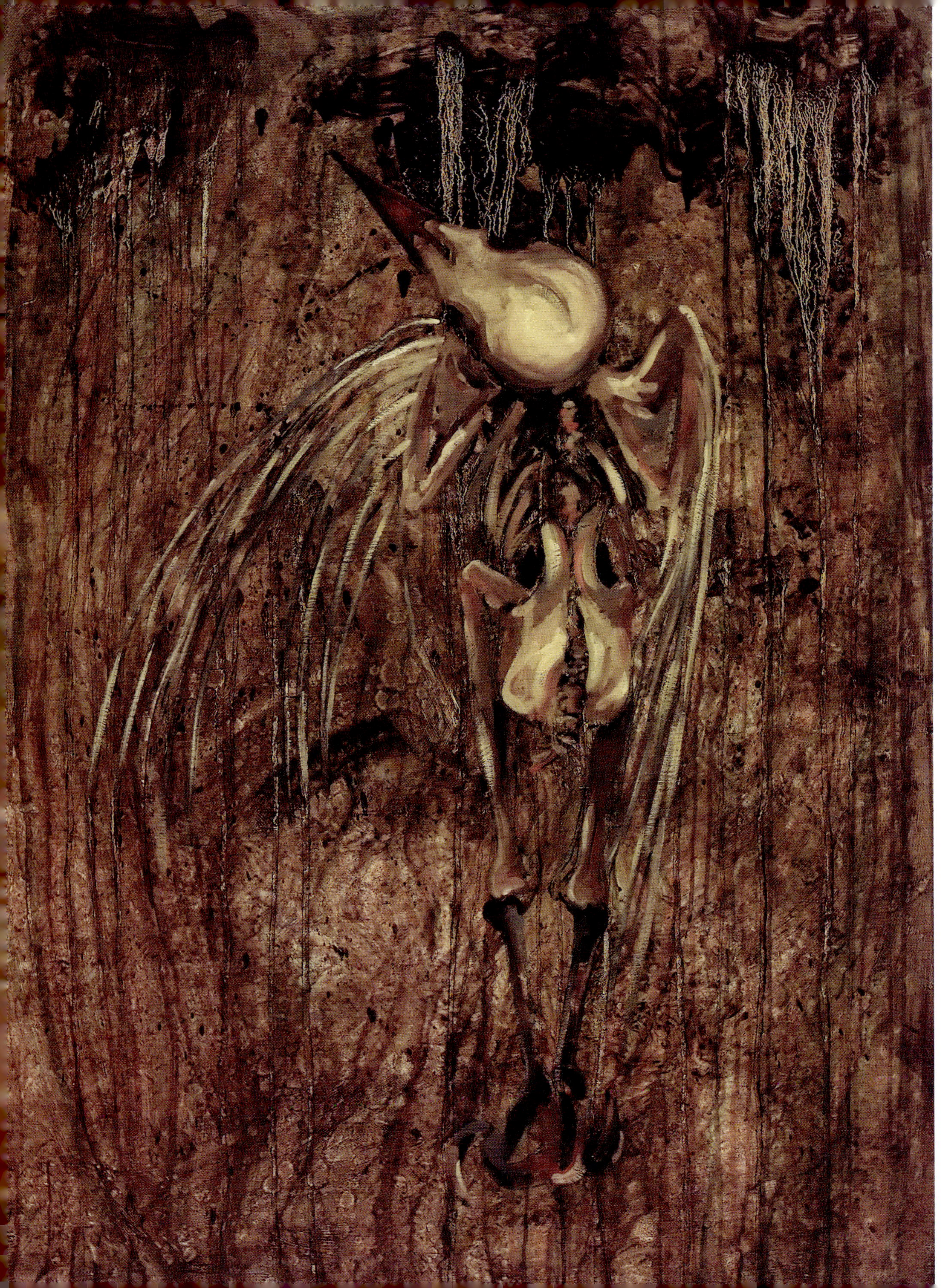

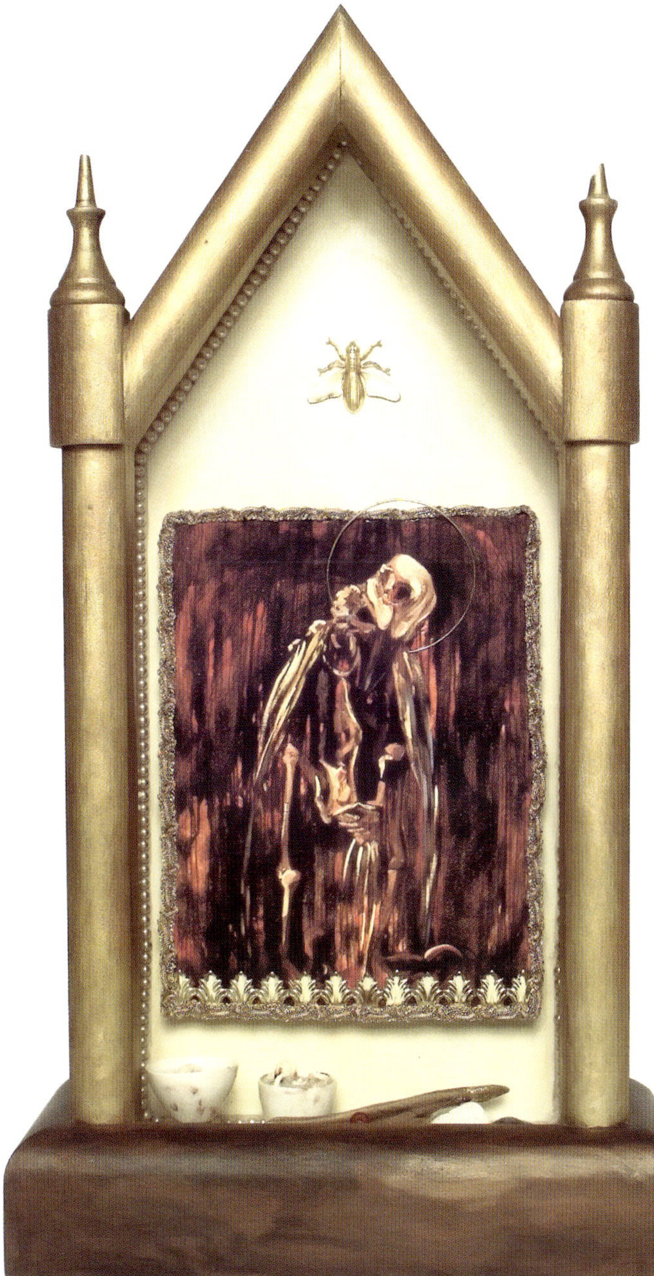

Cat. 44 *Untitled #1 (Red Beak)* 2000

Cat. 50 *Shrine* 2005

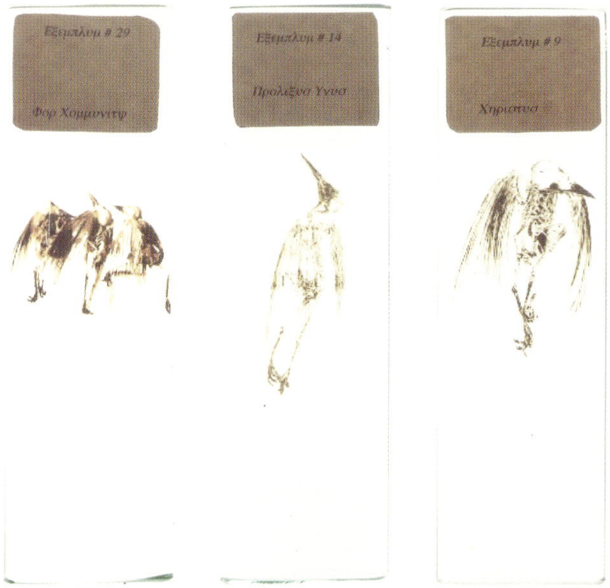

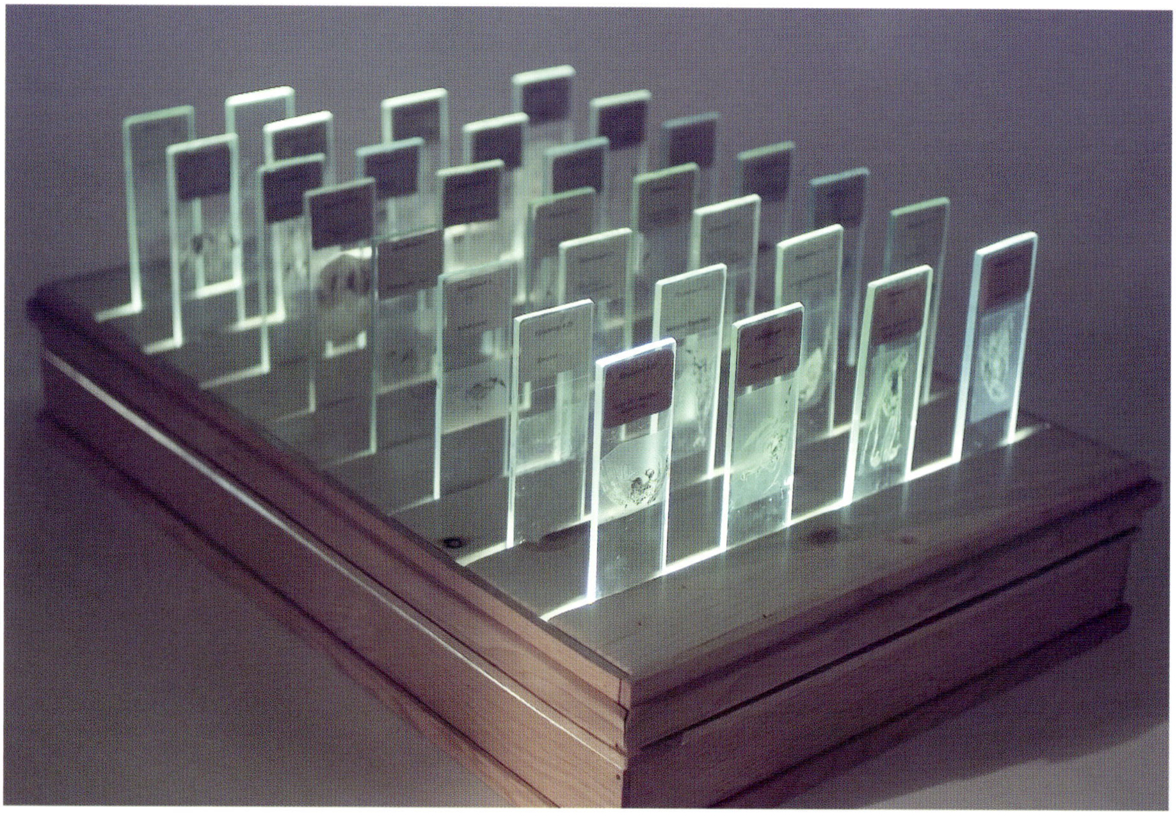

Cat. 49 *Slide Specimen Light Table* 2005

Cat. 47 *Untitled #4 (Knuckle Dragger)* 2000

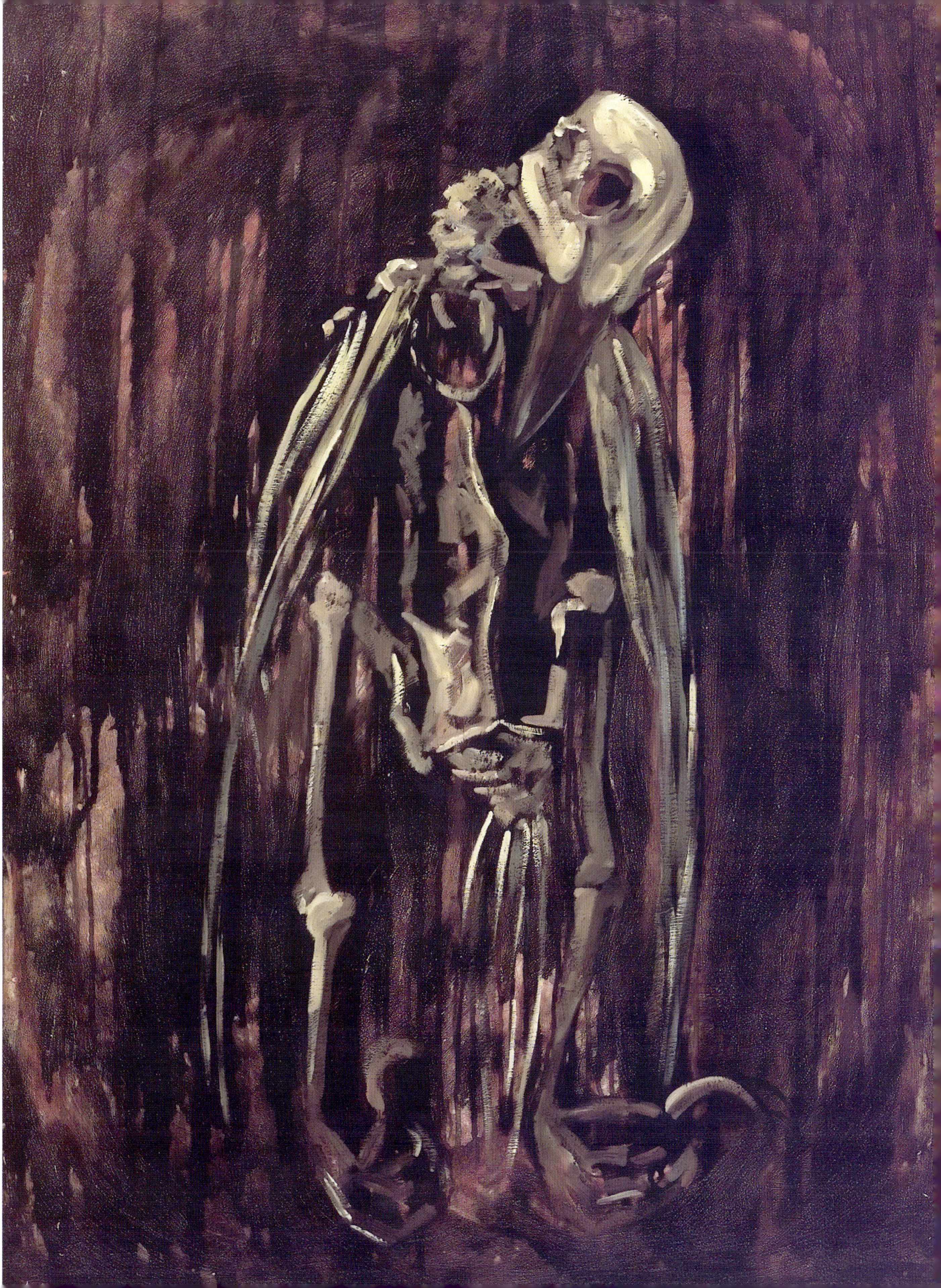

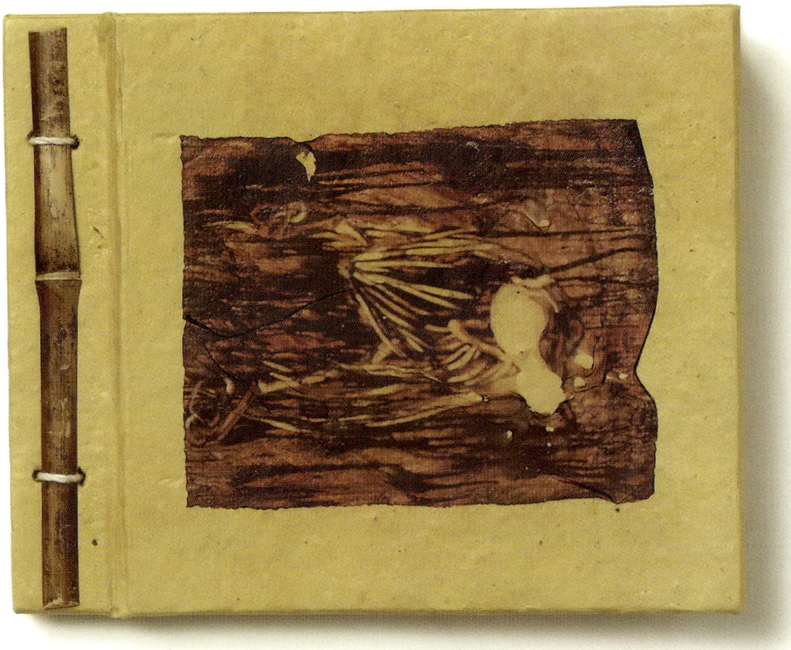

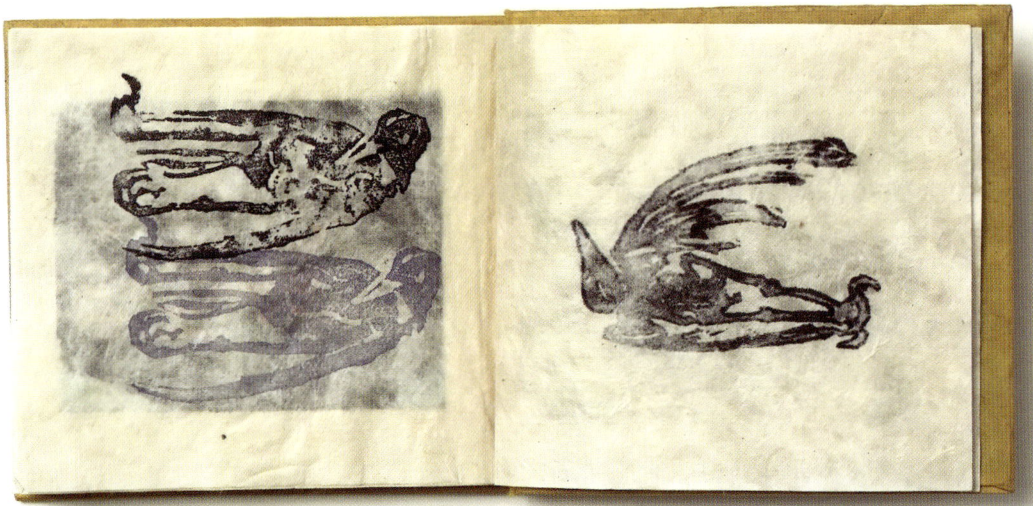

Cat. 40 *Untitled, Book #2* 2004-05

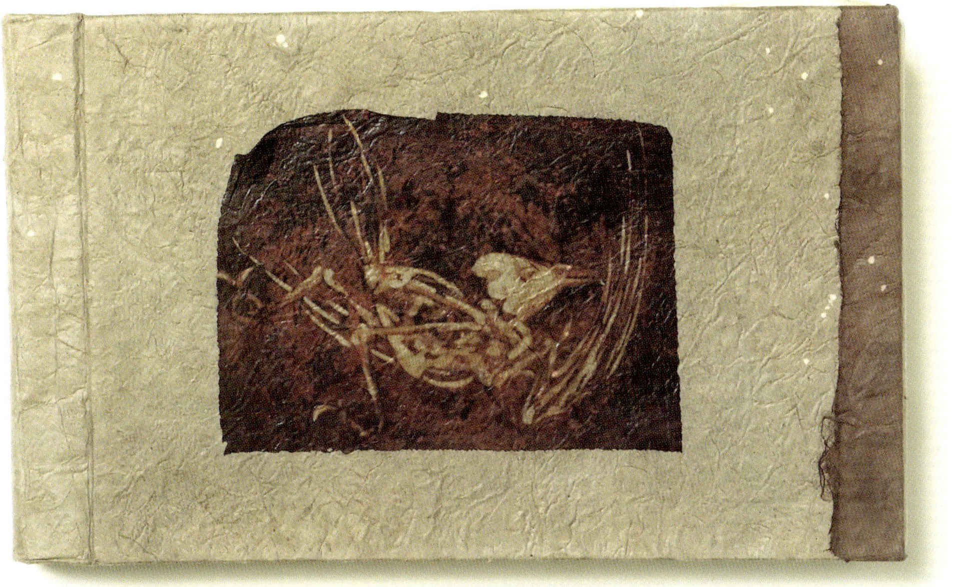

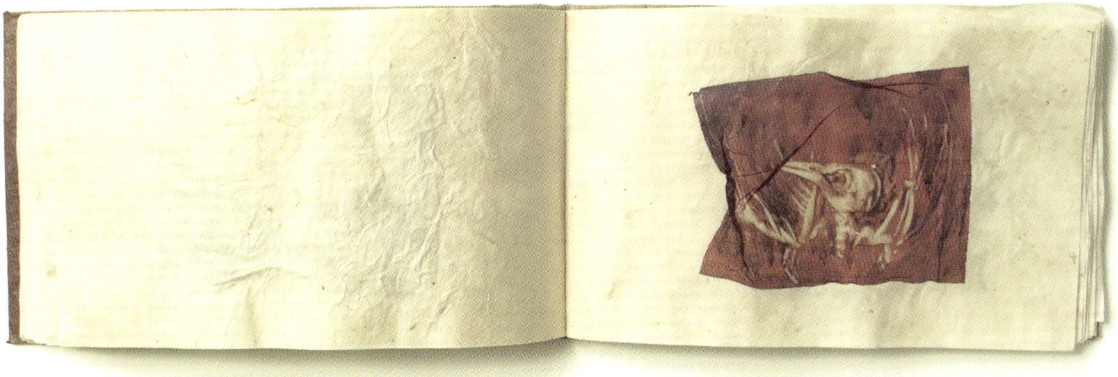

Cat. 41 *Untitled, Book #3* 2004-05

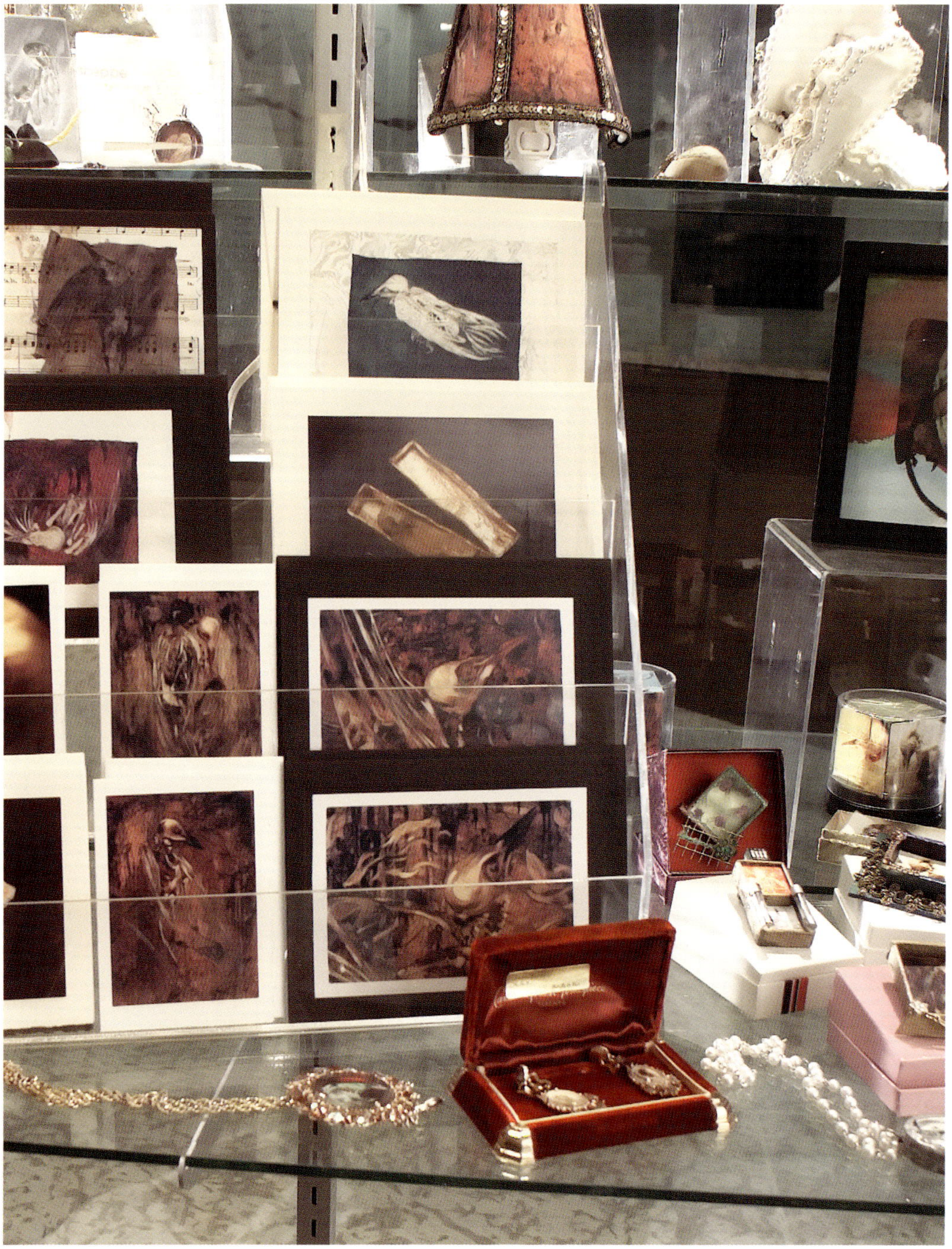

Cat. 51 *Gift Shop Installation* (detail) 2005

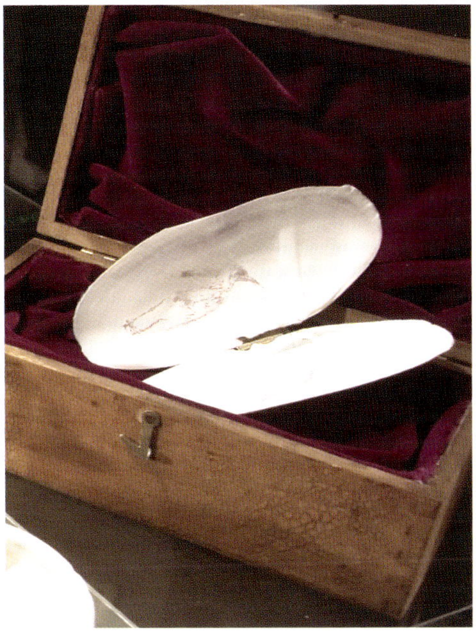

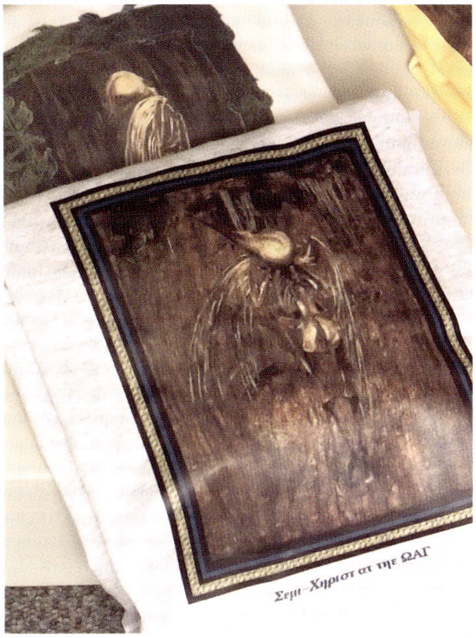

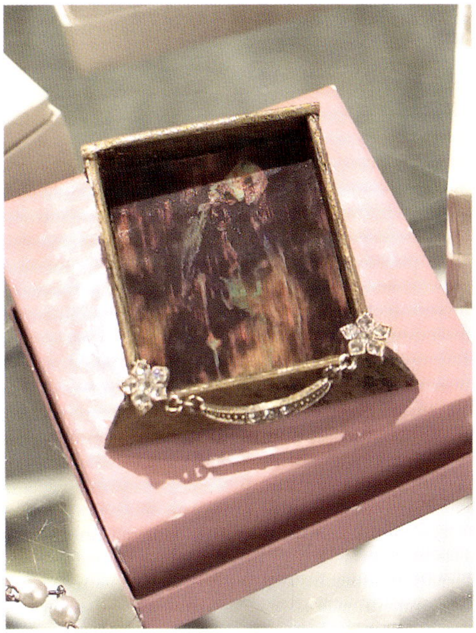

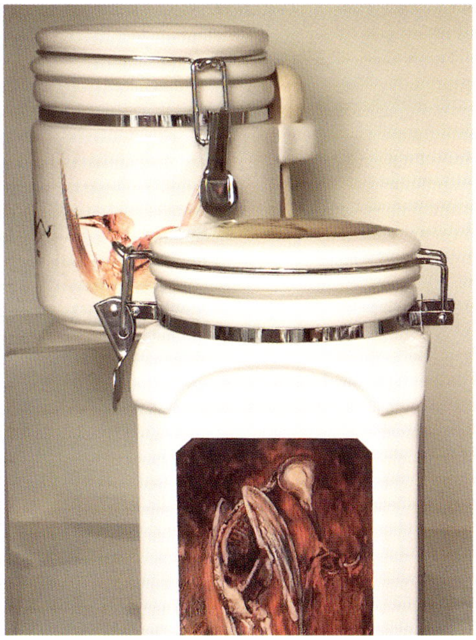

Cat. 51 *Gift Shop Installation* (details) 2005

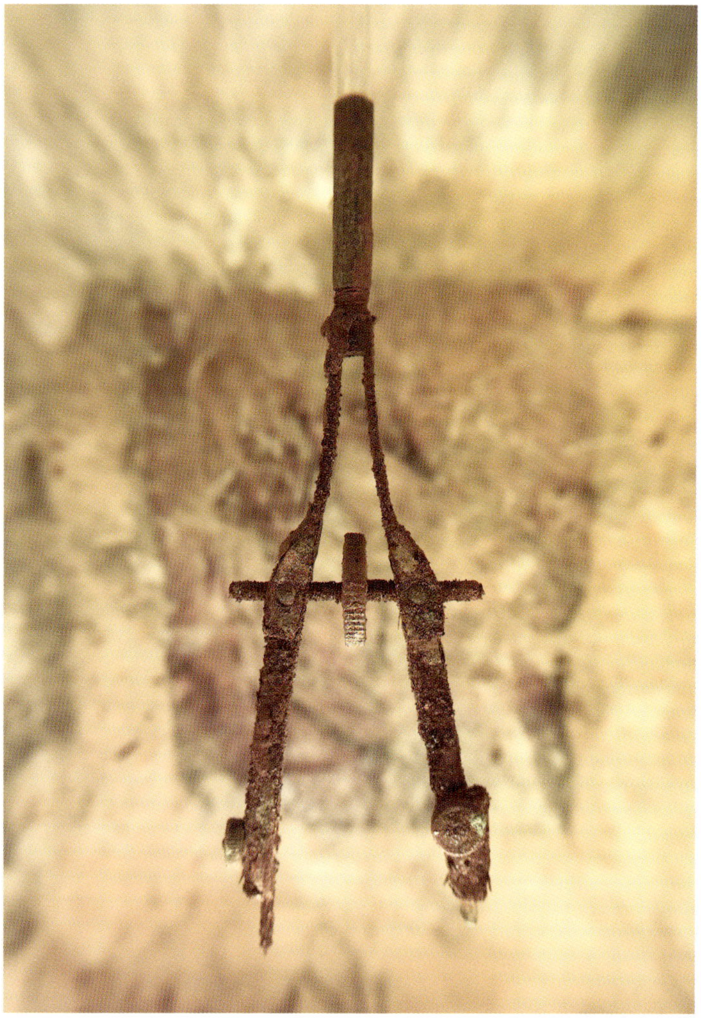

Cat. 20 *Untitled, Box #20* (detail) 2004

Works in the exhibition | Dimensions are height x width x depth

Cat. 1 *Untitled, Box #1* 2004
mixed media, 30.2 x 23 x 22 cm

Cat. 2 *Untitled, Box #2* 2004
mixed media, 25.1 x 17.8 x 17.8 cm

Cat. 3 *Untitled, Box #3* 2004
mixed media, 25.1 x 17.8 x 17.8 cm

Cat. 4 *Untitled, Box #4* 2004
mixed media, 25.1 x 17.8 x 17.8 cm

Cat. 5 *Untitled, Box #5* 2004
mixed media, 25.1 x 17.8 x 17.8 cm

Cat. 6 *Untitled, Box #6* 2003
mixed media, 25.1 x 17.8 x 17.8 cm

Cat. 7 *Untitled, Box #7* 2003
mixed media, 25.1 x 17.8 x 17.8 cm

Cat. 8 *Untitled, Box #8* 2004
mixed media, 30.2 x 23 x 22 cm

Cat. 9 *Untitled, Box #9* 2003
mixed media, 25.1 x 17.8 x 17.8 cm

Cat. 10 *Untitled, Box #10* 2004
mixed media, 25.1 x 17.8 x 17.8 cm

Cat. 11 *Untitled, Box #11* 2004
mixed media, 25.1 x 17.8 x 17.8 cm

Cat. 12 *Untitled, Box #12* 2004
mixed media, 25.1 x 17.8 x 17.8 cm

Cat. 13 *Untitled, Box #13* 2004
mixed media, 25.1 x 17.8 x 17.8 cm

Cat. 14 *Untitled, Box #14* 2004
mixed media, 25.1 x 17.8 x 17.8 cm

Cat. 15 *Untitled, Box #15* 2003
mixed media, 25.1 x 17.8 x 17.8 cm

Cat. 16 *Untitled, Box #16* 2004
mixed media, 25.1 x 17.8 x 17.8 cm

Cat. 17 *Untitled, Box #17* 2003
mixed media, 25.1 x 17.8 x 17.8 cm

Cat. 18 *Untitled, Box #18* 2004
mixed media, 25.1 x 17.8 x 17.8 cm

Cat. 19 *Untitled, Box #19* 2003
mixed media, 25.1 x 17.8 x 17.8 cm

Cat. 20 *Untitled, Box #20* 2004
mixed media, 25.1 x 17.8 x 17.8 cm

Cat. 21 *Untitled, Box #21* 2004
mixed media, 25.1 x 17.8 x 17.8 cm

Cat. 22 *Untitled, Box #22* 2003
mixed media, 30.2 x 23 x 22 cm

Cat. 23 *Untitled, Box #23* 2004
mixed media, 30.2 x 23 x 22 cm

Cat. 24 *Untitled, Box #24* 2004
mixed media, 30.2 x 23 x 22 cm

Cat. 25 *Untitled, Box #25* 2003
mixed media, 25.1 x 17.8 x 17.8 cm

Cat. 26 *Untitled, Box #26* 2003
mixed media, 30.2 x 23 x 22 cm

Cat. 27 *Untitled, Box #27* 2004
mixed media, 30.2 x 23 x 22 cm

Cat. 28 *Untitled, Box #28* 2004
mixed media, 30.2 x 23 x 22 cm

Cat. 29 *Untitled, Box #29* 2003
mixed media, 30.2 x 23 x 22 cm

Cat. 30 *Untitled, Box #30* 2004
mixed media, 30.2 x 23 x 22 cm

Cat. 31 *Untitled, Box #31* 2003
mixed media, 30.2 x 23 x 22 cm

Cat. 32 *Untitled, Box #32* 2004
mixed media, 30.2 x 23 x 22 cm

Cat. 33 *Untitled, Box #33* 2004
mixed media, 30.2 x 23 x 22 cm

Cat. 34 *Untitled, Box #34* 2004
mixed media, 30.2 x 23 x 22 cm

Cat. 35 *Untitled, Box #35* 2004
mixed media, 30.2 x 23 x 22 cm

Cat. 36 *Untitled, Box #36* 2004-05
mixed media, 25.1 x 17.8 x 17.8 cm

Cat. 37 *Community Box* 2002
mixed media, 4.4 x 12.7 x 40.6 cm
(contributing artists for interiors of 6 of the small boxes: Diane Whitehouse, Sheila Butler, Fay Jelly, Barb Flemington, Alison Taylor and Kai Wilbee)

Cat. 38 *Game Box* 2003
mixed media, 7.6 x 43.2 x 20.3 cm

Cat. 39 *Untitled, Book #1* 2004-05
mixed media, 15.2 x 12.7 x 5.1 cm

Cat. 40 *Untitled, Book #2* 2004-05
mixed media, 14 x 11.4 x 1.3 cm

Cat. 41 *Untitled, Book #3* 2004-05
mixed media, 11.4 x 19.1 x 1.9 cm

Cat. 42 *Ossuary #1* 2004-05
mixed media, 18 x 23 x 9.5 cm

Cat. 43 *Ossuary #2* 2004-05
mixed media, 16.5 x 22 x 10 cm

Cat. 44 *Untitled #1 (Red Beak)* 2000
oil, charcoal ashpaltum on plywood, 121.9 x 91.4 cm

Cat. 45 *Untitled #2 (Flinger)* 2000
oil, charcoal ashpaltum on plywood, 91.4 x 121.9 cm

Cat. 46 *Untitled #3 (Picker)* 2000
oil, charcoal ashpaltum on plywood, 121.9 x 91.4 cm

Cat. 47 *Untitled #4 (Knuckle Dragger)* 2000, oil, charcoal ashpaltum on plywood, 121.9 x 91.4 cm

Cat. 48 *Untitled #5 (Shrugger)* 2000
oil, charcoal ashpaltum on plywood, 121.9 x 91.4 cm

Cat. 49 *Slide Specimen Light Table* 2005, mixed media, 25 x 68 x 43 cm

Cat. 50 *Shrine* 2005
mixed media, 53.5 x 29 x 11 cm

Cat. 51 *Gift Shop Installation* 2005
mixed media, dimensions variable

This list will be constantly evolving as Shirley Brown is discovering new things about this lost civilization every day.

Shirley Brown's Biography

Shirley Brown is an established artist living and working near Deloraine, Manitoba. She has had solo exhibitions at aceartinc. (Winnipeg), the Art Gallery of Southwestern Manitoba (Brandon), Burlington Art Centre, and was part of The Winnipeg Art Gallery's *Manitoba Studio Series* in 1990. Brown has been in many group exhibitions at the Dunlop Art Gallery (Regina), A-Space (Toronto), and St. Norbert Arts and Cultural Centre, to name a few. In 1986 Brown participated in the Mentoring Artists for Women's Art (MAWA) advisory program. Since then she has twice served as a mentor with MAWA. She is part of a collective called the Coterie of Malcontents, and was recently a mentor to nine women artists living in the Southwest Region through the Rural Mentoring Group. Her work can be found in the collections of the Canada Council Art Bank, Manitoba Arts Council Art Bank, the Government of Manitoba, and various private collections.

Shirley Brown's Curriculum Vita

Education:

1987 - 2003 Workshops and/or classes with artists Graham Asmundson; Jan Brancewicz; Douglas Brolund; Sheila Butler; George Buytendorp; Aganetha Dyck; Martha Cole; George Glenn; Steve Higgins; Susan Mills; Diana Thorneycroft; Diane Whitehouse

1986 One-year mentorship with Diana Thorneycroft, Mentoring Artists for Women's Art Advisory Program, Winnipeg, Manitoba

Selected Solo Exhibitions:

2005 *Vestiges*, The Winnipeg Art Gallery; Art Gallery of Southwestern Manitoba, Brandon

2001 *The Ancient Ones*, Estevan Art Gallery & Museum, Saskatchewan

2000 *The Ancient Ones*, Art Gallery of Southwestern Manitoba, Brandon (brochure)

1995 *False Fronts*, W.K.P. Kennedy Art Gallery, North Bay, Ontario (brochure)

1994 *Queen Elizabeth I*, Woodstock Art Gallery, Ontario

1994 *Power Paintings*, Burlington Art Centre, Ontario

1993 *Recent Work*, aceartinc., Winnipeg, Manitoba

1990 *Studio Series*, The Winnipeg Art Gallery, Manitoba (brochure)

1990 *Tornadoes*, Art Gallery of Southwestern Manitoba, Brandon (brochure)

1990 *Tornadoes*, Medicine Hat Cultural Centre, Alberta

1989 *Tornado*, aceartinc., Winnipeg, Manitoba

Selected Group Exhibitions:

Upcoming 2006-2008 *In Your Dreams*, touring, Canada and Australia

2002 *Perspectives*, Surrey Art Gallery, British Columbia

2001-2002 *The Library Project* (curator/organizer/participant), toured, rural Manitoba and Gallery One One One, University of Manitoba, Winnipeg; Dunlop Art Gallery, Regina, Saskatchewan

1999 *The Winter of Our Malcontent: Coterie of Malcontents*, Kennedy Block, Brandon, Manitoba (catalogue)

1998 *Women Beyond Borders*, Dufferin Mall, Toronto, Ontario

1998 *Painting up a Storm*, A Space, Toronto, Ontario

1997 *Unfamiliar Ground*, Hartney, Manitoba (brochure)

1996 *Me, Me, Me & Me*, St. Norbert Arts and Cultural Centre, Winnipeg, Manitoba (catalogue)

1995 *Fractured Spaces*, The Winnipeg Art Gallery, Manitoba (brochure)

1993-1995 *Common Ground*, Manitoba Association of Community Arts Councils, toured throughout province (brochure)

1992 *Edge Manitoba*, Plug In Inc., Winnipeg (catalogue)

1991 *Mentoring*, The New Gallery, Calgary, Alberta (catalogue)

1990-1992 *Storm Warnings*, MacKenzie Art Gallery, Regina, Saskatchewan, toured (brochure)

1989 *Rural/Urban Landscape*, Main/Access, Winnipeg, Manitoba and Art Gallery of Southwestern Manitoba, Brandon (brochure)

Selected Awards:

2004 Major Arts Grant, Manitoba Arts Council

2000 Bridges Grant, Manitoba Arts Council

1998 Major Visual Arts Grant, Manitoba Arts Council

1998 Short Term Project Grant, Manitoba Arts Council

1997 Visual Arts "A", Manitoba Arts Council

1995 Visual Arts "A", Manitoba Arts Council

1993 Banff Centre for the Arts Residency Scholarship

1992 Canada Council "B" Grant

1991 Manitoba Arts Council Visual Arts Grant

1989 Manitoba Arts Council Visual Arts Grant

Selected Related Activities:

2004-2005 Mentor, Mentoring Artists for Women's Art, Winnipeg, Manitoba

2002-2003 Developed/Mentored, the Rural Mentoring Group with B. Flemington and F. Jelly. Mentored nine emerging artists from the rural area of Manitoba.

2002 Artist-in-Residence, Dunlop Art Gallery, Regina, Saskatchewan

1999-2000 Mentor, Mentoring Artists for Women's Art, Winnipeg, Manitoba

1997 Instructor, 5-day Art Retreat, Estevan, Saskatchewan

1994 A founding member of "Coterie of Malcontents" a group working for the artist-run concept in the south-west area of Manitoba

Selected Bibliography:

Brown, Shirley. *The Library Project*, 2001 (brochure)

Buchholz, Garth. "Queen Elizabeth I,.......the Prairie," *Winnipeg Free Press*, January 11, 1997 (review)

Dahle, Sigrid and Rushton, Al. *Rural/Urban Landscape*, Main/Access, Winnipeg, Manitoba and Art Gallery of Southwestern Manitoba, Brandon, 1989 (brochure)

Dahle, Sigrid. *Tornadoes*, Art Gallery of Southwestern Manitoba, Brandon, 1990 (brochure)

Dahle, Sigrid. "The Power and the Sorry," *Border Crossings*, Summer 1993 (review)

Dahle, Sigrid. *Me, Me, Me & Me*, St. Norbert Arts and Cultural Centre, Winnipeg, 1997 (exhibition catalogue)

Dahle, Sigrid, *The Winter of Our Malcontent, Coterie of Malcontents*, Kennedy Block, Brandon, Manitoba, 1999 (exhibition catalogue)

Froherk, Ron. "Town 'n' County," *Border Crossings*, Summer 1989 (review)

Gillmor, Allison. "Work Nourished by Places, Times," *Winnipeg Free Press*, February 18, 1995 (review)

Karlinsky, Amy. "Shirley Brown," *C Magazine*, Spring 1991 (review)

Karlinsky, Amy. editor. "Women and Humour," *Inversions*, Winnipeg, MAWA, 2002

Long, Timothy. *Storm Warnings*, MacKenzie Art Gallery, Regina, Saskatchewan, 1990 (brochure)

Lovatt, Tom. "Painting Out of the Blue," *Border Crossings*, Spring 1990 (review)

Madill, Shirley and Streifler, Lessa. *Edge Manitoba*, Winnipeg, aceartinc., 1992 (brochure)

Madill, Shirley. *Fractured Spaces: Contemporary Art in Manitoba*, The Winnipeg Art Gallery, Manitoba, 1995 (brochure)

McIlroy, Randal. "Tornado Series Provides Thrilling Ominous Vision," *Winnipeg Free Press*, December 9, 1989

McIlroy, Randal. "Brown Stirs Tempest like a Wild Tornado," *Winnipeg Free Press*, December 29, 1990

McKaskell, Bob. *Manitoba Studio Series*, The Winnipeg Art Gallery, Manitoba, 1990 (brochure)

McKaskell, Bob. *New Histories - The Manitoba Studio Series*, The Winnipeg Art Gallery, Manitoba, 1993 (exhibition catalogue)

Nelson, Diane. "Dead Birds Worthy of Reverence," *Brandon Sun*, May 24, 2000

Tivy, Sandra Vida and Ziemann, Sylvia. *Mentoring, Calgary: The New Gallery*, 1991 (catalogue)

Reid, Chris. *The Ancient Ones*, Art Gallery of Southwestern Manitoba, Brandon, 2000 (brochure)

Collections:

Canada Council Art Bank, Ottawa, Ontario

Manitoba Arts Council Art Bank, Winnipeg, Manitoba

Government of Manitoba, Winnipeg, Manitoba

The Manitoba Cooperator, Winnipeg, Manitoba

Private Collections

Artist's Acknowledgements

I wish to take this opportunity to acknowledge the many people who made this exhibition a reality.

I would like to extend my thanks to Jennifer Woodbury and Catherine Mattes from the Art Gallery of Southwestern Manitoba; Pat Bovey, Mary Jo Hughes, and Mary Reid from The Winnipeg Art Gallery; as well as the staff of these institutions who made this exhibition possible.

Thank you to Wayne Kilmury, whose carpentry skills helped me realize this dream of the "artifact" boxes. I also wish to thank Alwin and Kay Albrecht, who let me "play" in their pottery studio and who were so generous with their time and expertise.

Over my years as an artist, I have received much help from many people. I thank them all. During the production of this body of work I have received crucial feedback and "pearls of wisdom" from, among others, Steve Higgins, Diane Whitehouse, Michael Boss, Di Thorneycroft, George Glenn, and Cheryl Smith. Their support and insight has been invaluable.

I especially want to express my continuing gratitude to my fellow "Coterie of Malcontent" members, Fay Jelly and Barb Flemington. Without them, making art in our isolated area of the province would be far less enjoyable. Their ongoing encouragement, honest appraisal, and sense of humour are immensely important.

I thank friends from the artistic community and my local community who brought me items that they thought I might use in this work. Many such objects became "treasures" buried within the boxes.

I thank Murray Brown for his constant support and assistance. As well, I am grateful to Michelle and Keith Brown for their enthusiastic backing.

The financial support of the Manitoba Arts Council has made the production of this work possible.